ARE YOU JEWISH?

ARE YOU JEWISH?

◆

Five One-Act Comedy Plays
About Jewish Identity

Bruce J. Bloom

iUniverse, Inc.
New York Lincoln Shanghai

ARE YOU JEWISH?
Five One-Act Comedy Plays About Jewish Identity

iUniverse books may be ordered through booksellers or by contacting:

iUniverse
2021 Pine Lake Road, Suite 100
Lincoln, NE 68512
www.iuniverse.com
1-800-Authors (1-800-288-4677)

ISBN-13: 978-0-595-36123-6 (pbk)
ISBN-13: 978-0-595-80567-9 (ebk)
ISBN-10: 0-595-36123-4 (pbk)
ISBN-10: 0-595-80567-1 (ebk)

Printed in the United States of America

Contents

INTRODUCTION

Years ago, a New York bakery used to advertise its rye bread with the slogan, "You don't have to be Jewish to love Levy's," I always thought that catchphrase transcended mere advertising puffery. It was, I still believe, a profound truth. A tasty piece of bread is a tasty piece of bread, whether you're a Jew or not.

And funny is funny, whether you're a Jew or not. Yes, these five plays deal, in one way or another, with Jewish identity, so Jews in the audience likely can relate to these characters in more personal ways than others. But as I listen to the laughter at performances, and watch to see who's laughing, it validates my belief that you don't have to be Jewish to enjoy them.

Of course, it couldn't hurt, either.

These plays are easy to produce. The casts are small, and the production values are uncomplicated. Productions can be as elegant or as simple as your resources and inclinations permit. So long as the director and the actors pursue the basic truths of the stories, and create distinctive, true-to-life characters—rather than clichéd stereotypes—the plays will come to life for your group as they have for so many others.

If you're planning a full evening of theatre, rather than only a single one-act, consider two, or even three, of these plays. Any combination seems to work well together. Note that the character Arthur Kleinman is the protagonist of "Daniel Ortega And Those Yom Kippur Blues" as well as "Can You Ever Forgive Arthur Kleinman?" These two stories, together, make a solid full-length program.

Bruce J. Bloom
Southold, NY
2005

CAN YOU
EVER FORGIVE
ARTHUR KLEINMAN?

THE CHARACTERS

Arthur Kleinman, in his early 50s

Molly Kleinman, his wife, mid-40's

Rabbi Schatz, 91 years old

THE PLACE

A small, well-worn sitting room in the Workmen's Circle Home for the Aged

THE TIME

Saturday morning

As the lights come up, we see ARTHUR KLEINMAN and his wife MOLLY waiting in the sitting room.

MOLLY: So where is he?

ARTHUR: Services just ended, they said. He's coming.

MOLLY: How long have we been here?

ARTHUR: I don't know. Maybe fifteen minutes.

MOLLY: Oh, please. Half an hour, anyway.

ARTHUR: So if you know, why do you ask?

MOLLY: *(Looking at her watch.)* I'm just saying. We left the house at nine thirty, and it took, what, forty minutes to get here, then parking, and trying to explain to that woman at the desk, so it has to be at least…

ARTHUR: What difference does it make? We're here, and he's on his way, all right? I said I'd do it, and I'm doing it.

MOLLY: *(After a long pause.)* So where is he?

ARTHUR: He's ninety-one years old. Maybe he stopped to have his pacemaker recharged.

MOLLY: You'd think he'd be happy to have visitors. After all, who comes to see him?

ARTHUR: I'm sure I don't know.

MOLLY: At his age, everybody he knows is dead.

ARTHUR: Please.

MOLLY: You think he'll understand? I mean, when you explain to him?

ARTHUR: They said he's still reasonably sharp…lucid. But he tires easily, they said. Don't push him too hard. Well, we'll see.

MOLLY: *(After a very long pause.)* So where is he?

ARTHUR: *(Wearily.)* Ask me again. Go on.

MOLLY: I'm just saying.

> *Very slowly, RABBI SCHATZ moves himself in, in his wheelchair. He wears a yarmulke and a talis (prayer shawl). He stops, and regards ARTHUR and MOLLY warily. ARTHUR moves to the wheelchair, as if to help the old man move into the room.*

RABBI SCHATZ: Did I ask for help? Did I? I'll move by myself, thank you very much. *(With great effort, and at an excruciatingly slow pace, he moves himself farther into the room. ARTHUR and MOLLY watch his progress in silence.)*

ARTHUR: Sorry. I didn't know you...

RABBI SCHATZ: I'm not a...what is it?...an invalid, that I need done for me. Not yet. I get up in the morning, I shave, I dress, I go to the dining room. I told that aide she'll try to cut up my food for me, I'll cut off her arm for her. So who are you?

ARTHUR: Well...well...It's like this...

RABBI SCHATZ: You don't know who you are?

ARTHUR: I'm Arthur Kleinman, Rabbi Schatz.

RABBI SCHATZ: *(As if he recognizes the name.)* Ohhhh, Arthur Kleinman. *(A pause.)* I know you?

ARTHUR: I hope you'll remember. It's from a long time ago.

RABBI SCHATZ: I don't know any Klein. This is a mistake. *(He turns the wheelchair as if to leave.)*

MOLLY: Not Klein, rabbi. Arthur Kleinman. Tell him, Arthur.

RABBI SCHATZ: *(With a nod to MOLLY.)* And who is this?

ARTHUR This is my wife, Molly. You never met her.

RABBI SCHATZ: *(Again starting to leave.)* See? Her I never met. This is a mistake, I told you.

ARTHUR: No, no, please wait. I mean, I wasn't married when you knew me. I was just a boy. I was one of your bar mitzvah boys.

RABBI SCHATZ: Oh?

ARTHUR: You used to come to our house and give me Hebrew lessons when I was twelve years old. Kleinman. On Avenue A.

RABBI SCHATZ: Kleinman…on Avenue A. Right near Avenue B.

ARTHUR: Yes, that's right.

RABBI SCHATZ: Kleinman. A yellow house, was it?

ARTHUR: Yes! Yes, that's it.

RABBI SCHATZ: An up-and-down. You were upstairs.

ARTHUR: Yes.

RABBI SCHATZ: I remember schlepping up those stairs. On a hot afternoon, your mother would give me a cold bottle of beer from the refrigerator. That I remember, too. Well, you know, this is something, that a student of mine should come and see me after all these years. This is very touching. And you, too…what is it?…

MOLLY: Molly…Molly.

RABBI SCHATZ: Molly-Molly? What kind of a…

MOLLY: No, just…Molly.

RABBI SCHATZ: Ohhh. So, tell me, Arthur, what have you been doing since you were a bar mitzvah boy?

ARTHUR: Well, I went on and graduated from Franklin High. Then we moved out of the neighborhood. To Haddam Hills.

RABBI SCHATZ: Oh? With the fancy Jews in the big houses.

ARTHUR: Well, yes, I guess so. Anyway, I went to college, to Columbia. Studied economics. Then I took my masters at the Harvard Business School. I started working at Goldman, Sachs, but that really wasn't for me.

> *As ARTHUR warms to the telling of his story. RABBI SCHATZ's eyes begin to glaze over. Soon his eyes close and his head drops, his chin resting on his chest. ARTHUR is not looking at RABBI SCHATZ, and is unaware that the old man has fallen fast asleep.*

ARTHUR: The pressure was tremendous, and needless, I thought. I only stayed a year, and then I got a very nice offer from Citibank. I had thought banking was boring and stuffy, but Citibank is very progressive. They gave important responsibilities, right from the start, and that's the most important thing a company can…

MOLLY: *(She has been watching RABBI SCHATZ.)* Arthur.

ARTHUR: I'll get to it. Rabbi Schatz wants to know…

MOLLY: He's asleep.

ARTHUR: What?

MOLLY: He's asleep. Look at him.

ARTHUR: *(Turning to discover that RABBI SCHATZ is, indeed, asleep.)* He's an old man. What can I do?

MOLLY: Wake him up. We have to get on with this.

ARTHUR: I can't do that.

MOLLY: Of course you can. Just be very gentle, that's all.

ARTHUR: Oh, I can't.

MOLLY: He could sleep in that chair for hours. We have to do this. You agreed. Go on, Arthur, wake him up.

ARTHUR: *(He approaches RABBI SCHATZ carefully, reaching out hesitantly to touch the old man on the shoulder. In a whisper.)* Rabbi. Rabbi Schatz.

MOLLY: Oh, for God's sake. He's not going to break. Wake him up.

ARTHUR: *(A bit louder.)* Rabbi Schatz.

MOLLY: Let me do it.

ARTHUR: No, you can't. He's a very pious, orthodox man. He'd be scandalized if a strange woman started poking him.

MOLLY: Then go on. Just do it.

ARTHUR: *(Bending close to him. Now much louder.)* Rabbi Schatz.

RABBI SCHATZ: *(Suddenly his eyes open wide and he looks into ARTHUR's face.)* Arthur Kleinman, you rotten no-goodnik!

ARTHUR: Rabbi, you remember?

RABBI SCHATZ: You thought I wouldn't remember? That's what you thought, huh? Well, I don't forget you, not in forty years or a hundred years. What you did, what a stink you made, they should have put you in reform school, you nizik. And now you have the chutzpah to come here to me. Get out from my sight. And take her with you...what is it?...Molly-Molly.

ARTHUR: But Rabbi Schatz, I came here to apologize.

MOLLY: Yes, he's here to apologize.

ARTHUR: It's been on my mind all these years.

MOLLY: All these years it's been on his mind.

ARTHUR: Please hear what I have to say.

MOLLY: Won't you just hear what he has to say?

RABBI SCHATZ: Once isn't bad enough, I have to listen twice?

ARTHUR: *(He gestures MOLLY to be quiet.)* Rabbi, please hear me out. Give me just a minute.

RABBI SCHATZ: Give you? A slap in your face I'll give you. All the boys I taught Hebrew…must be two, three hundred, maybe a thousand…you are absolutely the only one to show such disrespect. To a rabbi, yet. Oy, just thinking, I'm so humiliated, so angry…

ARTHUR: You're right, you're right. I did a terrible thing. And I'm here now, forty years later, to ask you, beg you, to forgive me.

RABBI SCHATZ: It wasn't enough you refused to go through with it, just two weeks before your bar mitzvah day. You screamed out to the whole world that it was my fault. Could you believe it? My fault! *(Upset by the memory of the incident, he works himself up into a violent spasm of coughing.)*

ARTHUR: Rabbi, are you all right? Sit up. Take deep breaths. *(He becomes concerned as RABBI SCHATZ continues to cough. To MOLLY.)* He can't stop. What should we do?

MOLLY: I'll go call somebody.

RABBI SCHATZ: *(Between coughs.)* I need nobody. Who asked you to butt in? *(Finally, with great effort, he brings his coughing under control.)*

ARTHUR: You're all right?

RABBI SCHATZ: I'm a hundred percent, no thanks to you.

MOLLY: We tried to help.

RABBI SCHATZ: You want to help, then go away. I don't need you here I should be humiliated all over again. It wasn't bad enough you refused to be bar mitzvah after I worked so hard teaching you. But your grandfather, may he rest in peace, he was president of the shul...the Big Shul, yet, Beth Hamedresh Hagodel. That I should fail teaching his grandson, this was more than I...

ARTHUR: But Rabbi Schatz, I was just a child.

RABBI SCHATZ: And what kind of a child yet. A miserable...

ARTHUR: True, true, absolutely true. But I was only twelve years old. Is a twelve-year-old responsible for...

RABBI SCHATZ: You ridiculed me to the whole shul. Your grandfather...everybody.

MOLLY: But consider this, rabbi. A Jew does not become a man until he is bar mitzvah. So Arthur was just a...

RABBI SCHATZ: Oh, yes, really? You think I need a Molly-Molly to tell me about being Jewish?

MOLLY: No, I didn't mean that. I was just saying that until Arthur was bar mitzvah, he was still a boy, just a...

RABBI SCHATZ: He was *never* bar mitzvah. So...what? Now he's still a boy?

ARTHUR: No, I'm not a boy. I'm a grown man. But I was a child then. I thought as a child. I made a child's mistakes. Please don't continue to blame the man for what the boy did.

RABBI SCHATZ: *(With a deep sigh.)* Well...

ARTHUR: Rabbi, I know you're a sincere man, a compassionate man. I know you can find it in your heart to forgive something that...

MOLLY: It's in the best tradition of being a Jew that...

RABBI SCHATZ: Again you're telling me how to be a Jew?

ARTHUR: *(To MOLLY.)* Would you please? *(To RABBI SCHATZ.)* I'm here to tell you that I sincerely regret the things I said so long ago. And that it has been a great loss to me, all my life, that I was never bar mitzvah.

RABBI SCHATZ: *(After a long pause.)* Well, I suppose...

ARTHUR: Yes? Yes?

RABBI SCHATZ: All right. You were a child. A rotten child, but a child. And you did come here, to show your respect...and to clear your conscience.

ARTHUR: So you're willing to accept my apology?

RABBI SCHATZ: I suppose so.

ARTHUR: Oh thank you, rabbi, from the bottom of my heart. It's hard to express what this means to me. To be able to make amends after so many years...well, it's a blessing, that's what it is. You know, in our lives we don't often get the opportunity to...

RABBI SCHATZ: All right, all right.

ARTHUR: I'm just saying that...

RABBI SCHATZ: I forgive you. Genug. *(Pronounced geh-NOOG—means "enough.")*

MOLLY: *(Handing ARTHUR a box wrapped in gift paper.)* Don't forget this. *(To RABBI SCHATZ.)* We brought this for you. It's very special.

ARTHUR: *(Handing the box to RABBI SCHATZ.)* Rabbi, I hope you'll accept this.

RABBI SCHATZ: What, something for me? Why did you think…

ARTHUR: Just a token, a symbol of my respect.

MOLLY: Yes, that's all. Respect.

ARTHUR: Just to show you that I want to make up for the terrible way I acted.

MOLLY: He knows he acted terribly.

ARTHUR: I want you to have this so I'll know that after all these years, you accept my apology.

MOLLY: You accept his apology.

RABBI SCHATZ: All right, I understand already. Then you were pretty sure I was going to forgive you, yes?

ARTHUR: I was hoping.

MOLLY: Just hoping.

RABBI SCHATZ: So what is it? *(Very, very slowly, he unwraps the box, opens it, and unfolds the prayer shawl inside. ARTHUR and MOLLY watch silently, with growing impatience.)* A talis. You brought me a talis? I got already a talis. *(He touches the prayer shawl he is wearing.)*

MOLLY: This is a special talis. We got it in Jerusalem last month. It's from the Holy Land.

RABBI SCHATZ: So where do you think this one came from? Atlantic City?

ARTHUR: We thought you might like to have it, that's all. You see, we were in Jerusalem for a vacation, and I was explaining to our son Norris how sorry I was about being disrespectful to you, and how sorry I was that I never had a bar mitzvah. I told him I was buying the talis because I had decided to come and see you, and try to set things right.

RABBI SCHATZ: And your son, why were you telling him this? Didn't he know his father was never bar mitzvah?

ARTHUR: Well, yes, of course he knew.

MOLLY: He's always known.

ARTHUR: The truth is, he started to think that if it was all right for his father not to be bar mitzvah, then it was all right for him, too, and so...

MOLLY: *(Quickly, to ARTHUR.)* The rabbi isn't interested in the...

ARTHUR: No, this is the story. Why shouldn't he know?

MOLLY: Arthur, I don't think it's a good idea to...

ARTHUR: It's all right. Rabbi Schatz will understand. *(He begins pacing the room.)* Norris is a bright kid, you understand. But he's always been a bit of a rebel. Maybe he gets it from me, I don't know. Anyway, he was never really thrilled with going to Hebrew school. That's what they do now, they all go to Hebrew school. Nobody gets lessons at home any more. Well, Norris didn't like the teacher and he didn't like the other kids. So he came in a few months ago and announced he was finished. He wasn't going through with it…no more Hebrew school, no bar mitzvah.

RABBI SCHATZ has begun to fall asleep again. As ARTHUR talks, the old man's eyes slowly close and his head rolls back, his mouth open wide.

ARTHUR: Of course, we tried to explain how important it was to validate his Jewish identity, to tell the world who he was and what he believed. That's why we took him to Jerusalem. We thought it would…

MOLLY: He's asleep again.

ARTHUR: What? Oh.

MOLLY: *(Quietly.)* Just as well. It's a mistake to get into all this, Arthur. He's going to think we've come here just because it's what you had to do to convince Norris to go through with his bar mitzvah.

RABBI SCHATZ: *(Speaking with his head back and his eyes still closed.)* So that's what you want, Norris should be bar mitzvah. Some name for a Jewish boy.

MOLLY: What's wrong with wanting to make a bar mitzvah for our son? Is that so bad?

RABBI SCHATZ: *(Opening his eyes.)* No, go ahead. Invite all the fancy Jews from Haddam Hills, with the mink coats and the shrimp cocktails. You already gave the caterer a down payment, yes? And you printed the invitations with the little ribbons on them?

ARTHUR: So? We want to have a nice affair.

RABBI SCHATZ : So don't come here telling me how sorry you are about what happened forty years ago. What, you told the boy you felt so bad you had to come and apologize, it should be a lesson to him? That's it, isn't it? You're here so you can tell him you came. I don't understand why you bothered. Just tell him you were here, he wouldn't know the difference.

MOLLY: No. We would never do that.

RABBI SCHATZ: The Arthur Kleinman I knew would do it.

MOLLY: He was a child then.

RABBI SCHATZ: A leopard doesn't change his spots.

MOLLY: Look, we came. We're here.

RABBI SCHATZ: Him I understand, but why you? I couldn't understand why you were here, Molly-Molly. But now I figured it out. You were afraid if you didn't come along, he would never go see the old man Schatz. Because even now, he thinks what happened back then was because of me, because of what I tried to make him learn.

ARTHUR: Not so, that's not the reason. I was worried about my son. I didn't want him to make the same mistake I did.

RABBI SCHATZ: Tell me, Arthur Kleinman, can you still read Hebrew?

ARTHUR: What? Why?

RABBI SCHATZ: I just want to know, do you remember anything I taught you?

ARTHUR: I can read some. A little.

RABBI SCHATZ: But you still don't know what the words mean, right?

ARTHUR: No, all I can do is speak the words. But it doesn't matter to me now. Really. I don't want to get into the whole…

RABBI SCHATZ: No, you don't want to get into. But there was a time you screamed and you hollered. You had to know what every word meant. It wasn't enough for you to be able to say your prayers in

Hebrew, to say the words Jews have been saying for thousands of years. I'm the mean old rebbe made you sit there and struggle with words you couldn't even understand.

ARTHUR: *(Beginning to become upset.)* Look, Rabbi Schatz, that's all in the past. There's no reason we should open up things that...

RABBI SCHATZ: Why not?

ARTHUR: What will it accomplish?

MOLLY: *(Trying to avert an argument.)* We should be going, Arthur. We have to be at the...

RABBI SCHATZ: What it will accomplish is: I think you've forgotten why you disgraced me for no good reason. Oh, you were some awful kid. You had a mouth on you.

MOLLY: *(Desperately.)* We're going right now. We're finished here, and there's no reason to...

ARTHUR: Just a minute. There's something I have to say here.

MOLLY: Make it some other time. If you keep on with this, there's going to be a disaster.

ARTHUR: You may have forgotten a few things yourself, rabbi.

RABBI SCHATZ: I'm ninety-one years old. I'm entitled.

ARTHUR: Do you remember how you used to teach me at our kitchen table when I got home from school? You'd take our afternoon newspaper and you'd open it up to the crossword puzzle. I'd read aloud from the book, and you'd sit there and do the crossword puzzle. And drink beer from a bottle.

RABBI SCHATZ: It was hot in the summer. There was no air conditioning then.

ARTHUR: My lesson would last until you finished the puzzle.

RABBI SCHATZ: So what's the point?

ARTHUR: Do you really think you can teach a child that way?

RABBI SCHATZ: Not you.

MOLLY: Rabbi, thank you for your time, but we have to…

RABBI SCHATZ: You think you were such a brilliant student I should hang on every word? You had no interest, and no talent, either. Your kind of student I could listen to with half an ear. You gave me no great pleasure to teach you, and I gave you exactly the attention you deserved. With you, it was only the five dollars a lesson I got for being there. Nothing more.

ARTHUR: Do you hear what you're saying? You call yourself a teacher? How could you feel that way about a child? I was a student.

RABBI SCHATZ: And I'm a rabbi. To a rabbi, you pay attention. To a rabbi, you show respect.

ARTHUR: You have to earn respect. You don't get that with a crossword puzzle.

RABBI SCHATZ: So, Arthur Kleinman, it's getting clear to me. You didn't really come to apologize, because nothing has changed. You are the same as you were then.

ARTHUR: I did come to apologize. *(Seeing that RABBI SCHATZ is regarding him skeptically.)* Yes, I did. I figured, what difference does it make. He's an old man now, and I'm not getting any younger, myself. Why should this ancient argument continue to fester? I'll just say I'm sorry and be done with it.

RABBI SCHATZ: Even though I did the crossword puzzle while you read.

ARTHUR: Yes. Even though.

RABBI SCHATZ: That's very gracious of you, I'm sure. And you, Molly-Molly? You just want...what's his name?...Norris to be bar mitzvah so you can have your party. Isn't that why you came?

MOLLY: Maybe. I don't know. Yes, I want my son to be bar mitzvah, and I want all our friends and relatives to come and be proud of him. And I want to wear my new black dress. So shoot me. But I also know that I've heard Arthur tell the story about you and the cross-word puzzles a hundred times. And seen him get angry all over again a hundred times. Whenever I ask him to go to Friday night services with me, he remembers about you, and he won't go. I'm a religious person, rabbi, and believe me, it has been a frustration for me, all these years. I thought...I hoped...maybe today Arthur and you could finally put this business to rest. I can see that's not going to happen. But he did try. And, yes, Norris will be bar mitzvah on March 12 at Temple B'rith Kodesh.

RABBI SCHATZ: Oy, reformed.

MOLLY: Sorry.

ARTHUR: I guess there's nothing more. I'm sorry you don't accept my apology.

RABBI SCHATZ: But I did already. You didn't hear me?

ARTHUR: What?

RABBI SCHATZ: Did you ever know me to lie to you?

ARTHUR: No.

RABBI SCHATZ: That's because I always say the truth. I told you before that I accepted your apology. And that's that. I don't take it back.

ARTHUR: Well. I...I mean, I don't know what...

MOLLY: Thank you, rabbi.

ARTHUR: Rabbi, I just want to say that I…

MOLLY: *(Quickly.)* Arthur, it's time to go.

ARTHUR: Yes.

RABBI SCHATZ: But now there's something I got to tell you. You never listened to me then, but maybe now you'll listen.

ARTHUR: I'm listening.

MOLLY: He's listening.

RABBI SCHATZ: You know, it's never too late to be bar mitzvah. You, I mean.

ARTHUR: Well…

RABBI SCHATZ: No, don't answer. Take your time. Think about it.

MOLLY: He will. He definitely will.

RABBI SCHATZ: Don't forget, Arthur Kleinman, if you're going to be a Jew, you have to act like a Jew. It's what you do that's most important, even if you don't understand it all. There are always reasons. We survived, all these thousands of years, by being true to our heritage. Tell me, do you have your own talis?

   ARTHUR shakes his head slowly.

RABBI SCHATZ : No? Take this one.

MOLLY: That's yours. We brought it for you.

RABBI SCHATZ: I got, already. I don't need this one. But you do. Take it. Be well…and goodbye.

ARTHUR takes the prayer shawl from RABBI SCHATZ. RABBI SCHATZ turns, and with great effort wheels his chair slowly toward the door. MOLLY takes the prayer shawl from ARTHUR and arranges it carefully over ARTHUR's shoulders.

MOLLY: Rabbi.

RABBI SCHATZ: *(He stops and turns his wheelchair so he can see MOLLY and ARTHUR.)* Very nice.

The lights fade slowly to black.

DANIEL ORTEGA
AND THOSE
YOM KIPPUR BLUES

THE CHARACTERS

Arthur Kleinman, a 57-year-old Jewish man

Luis Valencia, a bartender from Nicaragua

Reesy Martinelli, a hooker

THE TIME

Now, nighttime

THE PLACE

The Four Aces barroom

At rise we see a dingy, dimly lit barroom on the edge of a declining section of a big city. The only patron is ARTHUR KLEINMAN, who is wearing a dark suit, white shirt and tie, and a yarmulke. He sits on a barstool thoughtfully sipping a glass of whiskey. LUIS, the bartender, is both amused and puzzled as he observes ARTHUR.

ARTHUR: *(Self-consciously, seeing that LUIS is watching him.)* Any pretzels?

LUIS: No.

ARTHUR: Potato chips?

LUIS: No.

ARTHUR: Some peanuts, maybe?

LUIS: No.

ARTHUR: Nothing at all, then?

LUIS: Only to drink. The management don't believe in food.

ARTHUR: I'll just drink, then.

LUIS: *(After a pause.)* You from here? Never seen you before, I don't think so.

ARTHUR: I've never been in here. Till tonight. But I used to live in this neighborhood. Over on Avenue A.

LUIS: Oh, yeah? No kidding. *(After a pause.)* You no Puerto Rican.

ARTHUR: Me? No.

LUIS: And you no Colombiano, I don't think so.

ARTHUR: No, I'm not from Latin America.

LUIS: Then I know it was a long time ago you live here.

ARTHUR: Must have been forty years ago. I was a kid. The neighborhood was Jewish and Italian then.

LUIS: You was one of the Jews, right?

ARTHUR: That's right. Still am.

LUIS: Is why you wearing that little Jew hat.

ARTHUR: *(Removing his yarmulke and putting it on the bar.)* Forgot I had it on. Not used to wearing one.

LUIS: Only when you come down to the barrio for a drink, right?

ARTHUR: Well, actually I…It doesn't matter. I don't want to bore you with this.

LUIS: Hey, is all right. Go ahead.

ARTHUR: It really doesn't mean anything to anyone but me.

LUIS: I care 'bout everybody. I'm a student of the human condition. I mean it. Ask anybody. *(Seeing that ARTHUR is regarding him suspiciously.)* You don't believe me?

ARTHUR: I didn't say a word.

LUIS: No, but I see how you looking at me. You thinking, how can this bartender from Managua be a true philosopher? That's what you thinking, right?

ARTHUR: No.

LUIS: Come on, you know that's what you thinking.

ARTHUR: Well, let's say I'm surprised to meet up with…such a dedicated student of the human condition…in the Four Aces bar.

LUIS: Luis Valencia is a surprising person. Ask anybody. So…tell me, Mr….

ARTHUR: *(After a pause.)* Kleinman.

LUIS: Kleinman. That's a Jew name, right? You got a first name, too, prob'ly?

ARTHUR: Arthur. My name is Arthur Kleinman.

LUIS: *(Mouthing the name.)* Arthur. Arthur. I can't say that too good. I gonna call you Artie. Easier to say, you know what I mean? So look, Artie, why you all dressed up with a tie and all, and a Jew hat, sitting here alone in a Latino saloon? *(Making a frame with his fingers and peering at ARTHUR through it.)* I mean, what's wrong with this picture?

ARTHUR: I'm on the run, and I'm hiding.

LUIS: No kidding. *(Picking up the yarmulke.)* What you do, Artie, hold up a Jew church?

ARTHUR: Close. Actually, I'm supposed to be *in* a synagogue right now. Temple B'rith Kodesh, over on Brightman Boulevard. You know it?

LUIS: With the big round window in front? Colored glass, and all? Yeah, I been by there. Ought to sell it to the Catholics. Not many Jews left around here, I don't think.

ARTHUR: Mostly they live in Parkview and Haddam Hills now, but they still come back. You know why? It's the old neighborhood. They want to be young again, so they come back for the High Holy Days.

LUIS: Oh, yeah. I read about that. Big-time Jew holidays.

ARTHUR: They remember how it was. They all called it The Big Shul then.

LUIS: Hot stuff, huh?

ARTHUR: Everybody went there. For years, my grandfather was president. In those days the men sat downstairs and the women sat in the balcony with the kids. I'd sit upstairs my mother, but then I'd get restless, so I'd go and find my *zaide*...my grandfather...who was with the men downstairs. The old guys with beards wore prayer shawls that smelled like the snuff they used. Once one of them gave me a pinch of snuff. I sucked it in, and then I sneezed so loud the praying came to a total halt and the whole congregation turned to stare at me. Funny what you remember.

LUIS: So you come back to be there tonight? What is it, one of those Holy Days?

ARTHUR: It's the start of Yom Kippur, the Day of Atonement. I was there tonight already...in the synagogue...for the first time in all these years.

LUIS: What, you walked out?

ARTHUR: It was hot and stuffy. I was bored. And I knew it was going to go on for hours. I told my wife I was going outside for some air.

LUIS: And you steer yourself right into a saloon.

ARTHUR: First one I could find.

LUIS: Shows a lack of religious commitment.

ARTHUR: The rabbi was so cold and overbearing. And all those prayers in Hebrew. I didn't understand it then and I don't understand it now. It was like walking into someplace I didn't belong, like I was a foreigner in a country where nobody really wanted me.

LUIS: *(Nodding knowingly.)* Imagine that.

ARTHUR: Coming back was a great disappointment.

LUIS: Yeah? What did you expect?

ARTHUR: The feeling that I'd come home. I don't know...a spiritual experience.

LUIS: You looking for a spiritual experience, huh? You know what you need, Artie?

ARTHUR: What?

LUIS: You drinking scotch now, right? That ain't gonna do it for you, my man. You got to have something to turn on your lights.

ARTHUR: And what's that?

LUIS: You one lucky person, you know that? I got answers for all kinds of problems, and I got one for the blues...what you call it again, this holiday?

ARTHUR: Yom Kippur.

LUIS: Yeah, I got a medicine for those Yom Kippur blues. Is a drink I call it the Ortega. I invent it back in Managua. Was a big favorite of Daniel Ortega. You heard of him? Big man in Nicaragua. Ortega, he used to come all the way across town for this drink of mine.

ARTHUR: On Yom Kippur?

LUIS: Man, you kidding. What does a Sandinista know about a Jew holiday? No, Ortega used it to focus his energy before he give a speech. Got to be where he don't get in front of a microphone without drinking a couple. I mean, he owe everything to me. Ask anybody.

ARTHUR: And what are you telling me...that you want to make one for me?

LUIS: Is what you need, Artie.

ARTHUR: No, I don't think·so. Actually, I'm not supposed to be eating or drinking anything. We're supposed to fast all day, from one sundown to the next.

LUIS: *(Pointing to the drink ARTHUR holds.)* Scotch don't count, huh? Or maybe God ain't looking for Jews inside Latino saloons.

ARTHUR: I never did go for the fasting. Gives me a headache. Got money in my pocket, too. That's another Yom Kippur no-no. But in my heart, I'm a Jew.

LUIS: In my heart I'm a bartender. Tell you what, Artie. You need help. I'm going to mix you an Ortega. No charge.

ARTHUR: That's really not such a good…

LUIS: No, listen, listen. I mix you one and you just taste it. If you don't think that you having a genuine spiritual experience, we just pour it out and forget about it.

ARTHUR: I have to get back to the synagogue, and I don't want to be…

LUIS: No problem, man. You get back there, you be so spiritual, you be a genuine born-again Jew.

ARTHUR: I don't know…

LUIS: Artie, you are a man who is lost. You sitting there on a barstool looking for you lost faith, and you don't know even where to start. Could be you never find it, unless I gonna help you. *(With solemn determination.)* I mix this Ortega for you, you find what you looking for. Guaranteed.

ARTHUR: *(After a thoughtful pause.)* How can I resist.

LUIS: *(As he begins taking down six or seven bottles from the back-bar, preparing to mix the drink.)* Listen, Artie, this going to be defining event in your life. You have your first Ortega, is a revelation, you know what I mean. *(Searching, then finding.)* Where is the dark rum? Oh, yeah.

ARTHUR: Just a taste, now.

LUIS: Absolutely. One taste is all it takes.

ARTHUR: Does all that stuff really go into it?

LUIS: Oh, yes. Is a very sensitive and delicate thing, the Ortega. Take me four years to figure out the right mixture exactly. Of course, I don't call it an Ortega in that time, because Daniel Ortega, he never drank one then.

ARTHUR: No? What did you call it?

LUIS: At that time, I call it a Pit Bull.

ARTHUR: Whoa, wait a minute…

LUIS: But that was before I put in butterscotch schnapps and peach brandy to mellow it out. Hey, trust me, Artie. In a few minutes you gonna be on top of the mountain, where you see everything…and understand everything.

> *ARTHUR watches intently as LUIS begins mixing the drink. LUIS works slowly, with great precision, measuring carefully as he pours liquids of various colors from the bottles on the bar into a shaker filled with ice. As LUIS creates the Ortega, it becomes clear from the number and the amounts of ingredients that it is a big, powerful drink.*

ARTHUR: *(Examining one of the bottles.)* I don't think I ever tasted tequila before.

LUIS: You ain't gonna taste it now, either. An Ortega don't taste like any of the stuff that goes into it. What do they say: the big thing is more than all the pieces.

ARTHUR: The whole is more than the sum of its parts.

LUIS: That's it. Just like life.

ARTHUR: Jews don't think that way. We're more concerned with the parts. You want to be a good Jew, there are lists of things you have to do, and things you're not supposed to do. They tell us there's a whole list of sins we have to atone for. Alphabetical, from A to Z. Abusing…betraying…being cruel…and on and on. You know what? I didn't do those things. Why should I atone for things I didn't do?

LUIS: No sins at all? You didn't do nothing?

ARTHUR: I really didn't.

LUIS: Come on, everybody does sins.

ARTHUR: I didn't commit any of the sins on that list.

LUIS: *(Shaking his head ruefully.)* You one sorry-ass dull guy.

ARTHUR: I'm afraid you're right. Sad, isn't it?

LUIS: Is not sad. Is pathetic. How old you are, Artie?

ARTHUR: Fifty-seven. Why?

LUIS: Like I thought, you not an old man. But still, you closer to the end than you are to the beginning.

ARTHUR: I suppose so.

LUIS: You don't just suppose so. You know it for sure. So now you think sometimes about when you going to die, right?

ARTHUR: Sometimes. My cousin died this summer, and he was only fifty. Makes you think. How much longer do I have? And would you believe, I think about God. Never used to.

LUIS: That's why you come back here to atone after forty years, Artie. I mean, you get scared maybe there really is a God, and He pissed off at you because you ignore Him all this time. You get older, you figure you better start believing. Old people homes full of religious old farts. *(He puts the metal top on the glass shaker filled with ice and liquor.)* Now, this is important. The shaking. Gotta be not too little, not too much. Six times is exactly right. *(He shakes the shaker.)* Uno…dos…tres…quarto…cinco…seis. You following this, Artie?

ARTHUR: Why? So I can make Ortegas at home?

LUIS: Nobody can make Ortegas at home. You want an Ortega, you got to come to Luis.

> *LUIS pours the drink, including the ice, slowly into a large brandy snifter, as ARTHUR watches in silent wonder as the drink fills the glass.*

ARTHUR: Is that all for me? That's a huge drink.

LUIS: Is only one basic Ortega, regulation size. Daniel Ortega, he drink two, mostly. Sometime even three.

ARTHUR: Well, I'm only going to have a taste. Of one. That was the agreement.

LUIS: Only what you want, Artie. You don't like how it tastes, you just spit it on the floor.

> *LUIS watches as ARTHUR lifts the drink, looks at it carefully, smells it, then finally takes a tentative taste.*

LUIS: Your whole life going to change, right now.

ARTHUR: Come on, it's just a…*(Savoring the aftertaste.)* That's…that's…

LUIS: That's what?

ARTHUR: Most unusual.

LUIS: Smooth?

ARTHUR: *(Taking another sip.)* Smooth.

LUIS: Tasty?

ARTHUR: *(Drinking more.)* It's wonderful. It doesn't even taste strong. But I shouldn't be drinking all this.

LUIS: Come on, Artie, don't be a stiff. I mean, if it feels good, do it. That's what I say.

ARTHUR: *(Drinking more.)* Never had anything like it.

LUIS: You start to feel enlightened yet? You feel a spiritual experience coming on?

ARTHUR: I'm really not…

LUIS: Is too soon, prob'ly. Give it a couple minutes. *(Pointing at the drink.)* Go on. Drink.

ARTHUR: *(He drinks more. Suddenly startled, he stops.)* Hey!

LUIS: What?

ARTHUR: Did you just turn up the lights?

LUIS: Ah. The room gets bright very quick?

ARTHUR: Yes…yes.

LUIS: Look like everything got a glow on it? Pink, kinda?

ARTHUR: *(With a profound sense of enlightenment, and a beatific smile.)* Yes, just like that!

LUIS: This is it, Artie. This the spiritual experience getting started.

ARTHUR: It's unreal.

LUIS: No, no, no…is the genuine article. Now you gonna see everything clear. You gonna be so happy, you wanna stand up and sing.

ARTHUR: Really? Did Daniel Ortega stand up and sing?

LUIS: He was a terrible singer. So he stand up and make a speech instead.

ARTHUR: Oh, come on.

LUIS: Ask anybody.

> *REESY makes a grand entrance into the bar. She is dressed in tight, brightly colored clothing, determined to be noticed. She is loud, punctuates what she says with laughter and is constantly in motion.*

REESY: She's stunning, she's voluptuous. Ha, ha. She's here because it's time for fun, time for joy. This is the place…and you're the man, Luis. *(Singing a makeshift song and moving about the room, with great drama.)* I love ya, baby…you got what I need…la da da dee dah…

ARTHUR: *(Staring at his drink.)* Will this always happen when I drink an Ortega?

LUIS: Her, you mean? No, no, she come in here a lot. Nothing to do with what you drinking.

ARTHUR: *(Drinking aggressively now. To LUIS.)* She's an appealing woman. *(To REESY.)* You're beautiful.

REESY: Ha, ha. This is a man of taste and judgment.

ARTHUR: I mean it. It's very clear to me. That pink glow.

REESY: I've got a pink glow, huh? *(To LUIS.)* Must be because I got such good news today. Ha, ha. Wait till you hear my news, Luis.

LUIS: Good news? What kinda good news you got?

ARTHUR: Good news is what we like. That's what we're searching for here.

REESY: Just listen to this. I'm going to be a model. I got a call from the agency this afternoon. They want me.

LUIS: No kidding. A model, huh? What you going to model?

REESY: *(Thrusting out her chest.)* What do you think? Brassieres, baby! Ha. ha. You ever see those ads for Victoria's Secret, with those gorgeous women slinking around in their underwear? Well, that's me now. I'm gonna be one of those Victoria's Secret women. For big money, Luis. Lotta money.

LUIS: How you get this job, Reesy?

REESY: I went to the model agency and the man said, "Let's see what you got." So I showed him, and he was very impressed. I mean, *really* impressed. Ha, ha. You know what he said to me? He said, "That's one of the best set of tits I've ever seen." Ha, ha. Isn't that something?

LUIS: Sure is.

REESY: Considering all the tits this guy looks at all day long. Ha, ha. I mean, it's really something, right?

ARTHUR: *(He has finished the drink. To LUIS.)* Say, where's the…

LUIS: *(Pointing.)* Just around that corner.

ARTHUR leaves for the men's room, leaving LUIS and REESY alone.

REESY: I mean, how about that? People all over America admiring Reesy Martinelli's boobs. I'm feeling really good. Ha, ha. You can understand why I want to celebrate, right?

LUIS: Oh, sure. You bet.

REESY: So what I need is three dime bags, Luis. Can you help me with that?

LUIS: Sure, I can do that.

REESY: Ha, ha. You're a sweetheart, Luis.

LUIS: Of course, you got the money.

REESY: Right now? Money right now?

LUIS: Gotta be a cash transaction. You know that. Ask anybody.

REESY: Look, I'm gonna be in the Victoria's Secret ads. Ha, ha. I mean, I told you my ship is coming in.

LUIS: Coming in don't buy nothing. Ship gotta be right at the dock.

REESY: Come on, Luis, don't you believe me?

LUIS: Is not a question of do I believe you. You want three dime bags, and a dime bag cost a dime. That's why they call it. So I gotta have the cash.

REESY: Look, I don't have thirty dollars just right this minute. Not at this very instant. But I am good for it. I have got a deal now. Big-time gig for a lot of money.

LUIS: Look, I love you plenty, but no way I can do this.

REESY: All right, I'll tell you what. I can get along with two bags, just for now.

LUIS: Can't do it.

REESY: One, then. One lousy bag, Luis. Just to tide me over. You'll get every penny, I swear to you. Victoria's Secret, for God's sake...

LUIS: Cash.

REESY: *(Losing it.)* You're a shit, you know that? *(Desperately backtracking, for fear of alienating LUIS.)* You know I don't mean that. You're my friend. But I'm gonna be sick. I mean, you know how it is.

LUIS: Sure I do. I feel bad for you. Say look, maybe I can help you.

REESY: *(Brightening.)* I knew I could count on you. Two bags, OK? Or…only one, if that's all…

LUIS: No, no, you got it wrong. I can't do credit. But I know a way you can get the money quick.

REESY: What? What do I have to do?

LUIS: No big deal. This guy drinking here, Artie, is Jewish guy prob'ly got a pocket full of money. And he feeling very confuse right now, cause he looking for something and he don't find it.

REESY: Yeah? What is he looking for?

LUIS: Something for him to believe in. Maybe some*body*…like you. See, trouble is, he afraid to get old and die some day. He ain't getting no help from God right now, so he looking. He pay you whatever you want, I think.

REESY: I don't want to do that any more, Luis. I mean, I'm going to model for Victoria's Secret…

LUIS: But that's…when?…next week, prob'ly. Look, what difference? Is just one last trick, for old time sake. Easy solve you problem.

REESY: But I have to get out of that.

LUIS: And you going to. This you last, final trick, absolutely. Hey, I bet he give you hundred bucks, easy.

REESY: You think so? A hundred?

LUIS: Good-lookin' woman like you? Model and all? A hundred no problem. And for a hundred I give you *ten* dime bags. No, *eleven*. I make him special drink and he's flying now. He think you some kinda saint. Hey, he's coming back now. Tell him you wanna dance with him.

ARTHUR: *(Returning to the bar.)* I've figured it out, just as you said I would. The ideas in my mind have never, ever been so lucid, not in my whole life.

LUIS: Yeah, lucid.

ARTHUR: I'm quite secure now that I have done no transgressing, and I there's absolutely no reason for me to feel guilty. I know it and God knows it.

LUIS: And now Luis Valencia knows it, too.

ARTHUR: I'm a good man. I lead a good life. I'm kind and I'm decent and I respect other people. That is quite enough for any man.

LUIS: Reesy here, she know you a good man right away. She tell me she like you.

ARTHUR: Reesy. That's an unusual name.

REESY: It's not a real name. It's short for Theresa.

ARTHUR: Reesy. Sounds like something a young kid would say. That was what your little brother or sister called you. Am I right?

> *LUIS turns on the radio. Hot Latin music fills the barroom. It is loud and brassy, with an insistent beat.*

REESY: *(A few provocative dance steps.)* Hey, I like this music. You want to come dance with me?

ARTHUR: *(Persisting.)* Am I right? Was it a brother or a sister?

REESY: *(Reluctantly.)* It was my sister. *(Pulling him by the hand.)* Come on, dance with me.

ARTHUR: I haven't danced in ten, fifteen years. This music...I don't know how.

LUIS: Look, I show you. You watch me, and then you do what I do, OK? *(He comes out from behind the bar and does an energetic dance with REESY.)* You do like this. Then like this. Now watch this. You turn her around. You feel the beat. You let yourself go. *(LUIS dips REESY precariously.)* Is your turn now. Go ahead, hold her.

ARTHUR: I can do this. I know I can do it. I can do anything. *(He assumes the classic ballroom dancing position, with his right arm around REESY's waist, and holding her hand with his left hand.)*

LUIS : No, no, lemme show you. You start like this. Take you hands and put them right here. *(He places ARTHUR's hands on REESY's hips.)* OK, now you dance. And while you dancing, I make another Ortega for you.

ARTHUR: Another one?

> *LUIS returns behind the bar to mix another drink, as ARTHUR and REESY dance to the music. At first ARTHUR is stiff and self-conscious, but, encouraged by both LUIS and REESY, he loosens up and begins dancing with abandon. What he lacks in grace, he makes up for in enthusiasm.*

REESY: Listen to the music. Ha, ha. Go with it.

ARTHUR: Like this? Is this good?

LUIS: Loosen yourself up, Artie. Is supposed to be for fun. Not for Yom Kippur.

REESY: That's it. Let yourself go.

ARTHUR: I told you. I can do anything.

LUIS: That's the way. Now you got it.

ARTHUR: I knew I could!

LUIS: You one terrific dancer, Artie.

> *ARTHUR turns REESY with a flourish as the music ends. Then he drops onto a barstool, breathing heavily.*

LUIS: See? Dancing is a spiritual experience…if you doing it right. *(Shaking the Ortega.)* Uno…dos…tres…quatro…cinco…seis.

ARTHUR: I'm not even tired. Was I good? I was good, wasn't I?

REESY: You never did that kind of dancing before? Ha, ha. I can't believe it.

ARTHUR: This is some night, huh?

LUIS: And you know what? Is not over yet. *(Setting the Ortega on the bar in front of ARTHUR.)* You have another Ortega, you able to do all kinds of things you never knew. You learn more here than you do in some Jew church, I bet. *(With a wink at REESY, he leaves for the back room.)* I go get some more rum.

REESY: *(To ARTHUR.)* So, you're feeling good.

ARTHUR: *(He takes a big swallow of the drink.)* Good doesn't begin to describe it. Strong and happy. Fit and capable. Kindly. Honest. Upright. *(A pause.)* Blameless.

REESY: Ha, ha. All that, huh?

ARTHUR: It's finally clear to me. I have nothing to atone for. I don't have to stand there with a prayer shawl around my neck, saying words I don't understand and begging God to forgive me for things I haven't done.

REESY: What?

ARTHUR: Never mind. It doesn't matter. Just say I finally understand God put us on this earth to…well, to dance and be cheerful. It's very simple and very clear. Don't you think so?

REESY: You're right. We should be cheerful. And here's a gorgeous idea for you. We could be cheerful together, at my place.

ARTHUR: What are you saying?

REESY: I'm just saying we could have ourselves a real party, you and me. We get a bottle, some nose candy. Ha, ha. What do you say? Be a night to treasure. Only cost a hundred, that's all. Because I like you.

ARTHUR: But you're a model, right?

REESY: Yes, I am. Of course I am. But, look, I have expenses. There's food…clothes…

ARTHUR: And the rent, I suppose.

REESY: No, not rent. I own a little house on Avenue D, all paid for. Grandma Lombardo, she left it to me. But of course there's heat…taxes. *(Touching his face seductively.)* Let's go. Give me a hundred, and I'll get what…

ARTHUR: Oh, I can't do that. No, I've never done that.

REESY: But I have a pink glow all around me. Ha, ha. Doesn't that tell you something?

ARTHUR: What?

REESY: *(Stuck for an answer.)* Well…ha, ha. You and me…Tonight… It's…gonna be great, that's all.

ARTHUR: I'm sorry, the answer is no.

REESY: *(Desperately.)* Well, yeah, maybe a hundred is a little steep. Tell you what, we can get it on for fifty, because I like dancing with you so much. That's the biggest bargain you're ever gonna...

ARTHUR: I can't.

REESY: *(Now in a panic.)* Thirty dollars. I have to have thirty. That's the best I can do. Give me the thirty now, and we'll go...

ARTHUR: It's not the money. I just would never do that.

REESY: I'M A MODEL FOR VICTORIA'S SECRET, FOR CHRIS-SAKES! A guy your age...do you think you will ever again in your whole life have the chance to make it with...

ARTHUR: Please don't go on. Why do you do this, Reesy? You're so beautiful.

REESY: *(After a long, sobering pause.)* Why? *(Another pause.)* Because life is sad and strange. And I gotta have help to get through it.

ARTHUR: What? Dope, you mean? Why?

REESY: If I tell you, will you help me?

ARTHUR: *(After a pause.)* Yes.

REESY: It's like a story in a book. *(Pause.)* February the fourth, nineteen years ago. Icy winter night. My parents went out to a movie and left me to watch my little sister. Her name was Jeannine and she was six years old. She's the one who used to call me Reesy. "Reesy, will you take me for ice cream?" "Reesy, can I sleep in bed with you?" She was a sweetheart, that kid. Well, I was sixteen, and when Ron Silveri called that night could he come over, I said yes. See, he was a handsome Italian guy with dark eyes and curly black hair, and all the girls knew he was a hot number. And I thought how lucky I was he was coming for me. I let him in the apartment, and right away we were touching each other...you know...and it was clear where it was going. But there was Jeannine, watching us. So he said, "I got my car outside. Let's go out for a few minutes." See, he was eighteen, and he had an old Pontiac...dark blue, it was. So I told Jeannine I'd be right back, and Ron and I went down to the car and got in. It was so cold, but we didn't care. And while he was pulling off my pants in the back seat...(*Long pause.*). Jeannine somehow turned on the gas on the stove upstairs, and a newspaper that was laying there caught on fire, they said, and right away the whole kitchen started to go up. Me and Ron were getting out of the car when we heard somebody yell fire. We ran up the stairs, but the smoke was so black and thick in the hallway, we couldn't get through. When they found her... (*Pause.*) What I had done was this: I traded my little sister for a piece of Ron Silveri.

ARTHUR: What a tragedy.

REESY: That's not the end of it. My father, he was a hothead anyway, and when it came out how it happened, he never spoke to me again, not one word, not even on his deathbed. My mother, she would've forgiven me, but she was afraid not to go along with him. I couldn't live with them any more, so I went with my grandmother, in the same house I'm still living in. By the time I was nineteen my grandmother was gone...and I was hooked. (*Pause.*) The face of that beautiful little kid haunts me every single day. Only sometimes I just can't deal with it. That's why I need thirty dollars so bad. I'm broke, and I'm drowning. (*In desperation.*) Help me.

ARTHUR: Look, that's no answer. You just can't keep on...

REESY: No, please. You're going to tell me about getting out...taking charge of my life...all that. No. There's only one thing you can do for me, believe me. Give me thirty dollars.

ARTHUR: I don't think...

REESY: Please.

> *ARTHUR stares at her in silence. Then he slowly reaches into his pocket, withdraws his wallet and takes out some money, which he hands to REESY.*

REESY: *(After a long pause, her face brightens, and she calls loudly to LUIS.)* Hey, where are you? Get in here, Luis, you got some heavy business to take care of. Ha, ha. *(She throws the money on the bar.)*

ARTHUR: What? You get that stuff from him?

REESY: Good stuff, too. Always. You have to be careful. *(Calling.)* Hey, bartender…ha, ha…are we gonna rock and roll, or what?

LUIS: *(Returning and going behind the bar. Seeing the money.)* This your thirty, Reesy? Or it's his?

ARTHUR: The money is hers.

REESY: You heard the man. My money. Thirty. Three dimes.

LUIS: Hey, let's keep it a little quiet, you know.

REESY: There's no secrets here. He knows all about everything. Three dimes, Luis, and I gotta go.

> *LUIS gives REESY three small, transparent envelopes filled with white powder, and takes the money from the bar.*

REESY: *(To LUIS.)* You're a good man. Ha, ha. *(To ARTHUR.)* And you're a good man. Thanks.

ARTHUR: It doesn't have to be this way.

REESY: Yes it does. *(She gets up to leave.)*

LUIS: We look for you in those brassiere ads.

REESY: *(She kisses ARTHUR on the cheek, then moves away from him and does a dance step.)* Come back again. We'll dance some more. *(She leaves.)*

LUIS: So, you give her that money for free, huh? She don't give you nothing?

ARTHUR: She seemed to need it.

LUIS: She always need it. To buy dope.

ARTHUR: And you supply the dope.

LUIS: That's what I do. I supply. Ask anybody. Hey, don't get so crazy serious. Is just another street whore. We got plenty come here. You need more Ortega, I think. Come on, I make you another one. *(He begins mixing.)*

ARTHUR : Doesn't it bother you, to see what she's become?

LUIS: Look, Artie, Is not my fault. She tell you that story about her little sister?

ARTHUR: Yes. Is it true?

LUIS: Sure, I think. She tell everybody, all the time.

ARTHUR: She's beating herself to death.

LUIS: She try to make up for her sin, that's all. She gotta…what you say?…make atonement.

ARTHUR: That's some guilt she carries around with her.

LUIS: Everybody got sins to carry around. You can't live in this world without doing sins.

ARTHUR: I don't know, I was sitting there in the synagogue tonight, and I couldn't think of anything sinful I'd done.

LUIS: Oh, come on. Ha, ha. You haven't even been in here an hour, and look what you done already.

ARTHUR: What?

LUIS: Well for one thing, you dance with a whore on a holy day. That gotta count for something so you can make atonement.

ARTHUR: You're right.

LUIS: And then you take money out of your pocket to buy dope. How about that, too? But hey, don't make yourself crazy. A little sin won't kill you. I think maybe is good for you. *(Shaking the Ortega.)* Uno…dos…tres…quatro…cinco…seis. *(He pours the drink into a glass and places it on the bar in front of ARTHUR.)*

ARTHUR: No thanks. No more Ortegas. No more pink glow. You'll have to drink it.

LUIS: No, I don't do that.

ARTHUR: Why not?

LUIS: Because I'm a supplier. I don't drink. I don't shoot up. I supply.

ARTHUR: I have to go now, Luis.

LUIS: You going back to the Jew church, right? Maybe pray a little before the night is over?

ARTHUR: You think so?

LUIS: Sure. Also, you gonna go get your wife.

ARTHUR: Goodbye, Luis. Thanks for the Ortegas, and the sin.

LUIS: I only make the Ortegas for you. The sin, you gotta make that for yourself. No problem.

ARTHUR: Yes. It's easier than I thought.

LUIS: *(He watches as ARTHUR leaves. Then he notices ARTHUR's yarmulke on the bar. He picks it up, and coming around the bar to open the door to the street, he calls after ARTHUR, holding the yarmulke high.)* Hey, Artie, you forgot your little Jew hat.

    Blackout.

THE BEST MEAL
YOU EVER ATE

THE CHARACTERS

Avram, a survivor

Netti, his wife, also a survivor

Jean-Paul, a chef

THE PLACE

The ghetto

THE TIME

The war

The lights fade up to reveal a room on the second floor of a war-shattered apartment house in the ghetto. The windows are broken. The walls are pocked with bullet holes. Only a few furnishings—including a small table and a few chairs—still remain. AVRAM and NETTI are watching the street below through a broken window. AVRAM has a rifle. We hear a long exchange of rifle and machine-gun fire, followed by the explosion of an artillery shell. Then there is silence.

NETTI: Stopped.

AVRAM: Wait.

They listen expectantly, but the shooting does not resume.

NETTI: No.

AVRAM: *(Hopefully.)* They're waiting. If they can avoid the Germans till dark, they'll get through the night. That's why they stopped shooting. Don't want to draw fire.

NETTI: No, wrong. That explosion. Artillery shell. Nazi bastards got tired of playing with them. Blasted them out.

AVRAM: You're so sure? You think they're…?

NETTI: Absolutely.

AVRAM: Maybe there's a chance that…

NETTI: No.

AVRAM: *(After a long pause.)* Then we're the only ones left. There were so many thousands. We're the last of thousands.

NETTI: What difference, a few dumb Jews more or less? Thousands, hundreds, a dozen. Now…

AVRAM: Now there are two. And I've never thought of myself as a dumb Jew, thank you.

NETTI: No, that you never thought, mister professor…mister *assistant* professor, actually. Nevertheless, you are a dumb Jew. We're both dumb Jews. Because here we are, in the end. This…this is really stupid. Idiotic. Asinine. Absurd.

AVRAM: You forgot ludicrous.

NETTI: Forgive me if I've lost my edge. Something about hunger makes me dull. What an ending.

AVRAM: There's profound meaning here. Some day they'll write songs about us. We made a statement.

NETTI: Some statement. My God, any Jew with half a brain spent his life scheming how to get out of this vile slum. But this pack of fanatics…we had to pick this place to…

AVRAM: The ones who didn't…

NETTI: We had to pick the ghetto to make our statement.

AVRAM: The ones who didn't…

NETTI: You don't know. The ones they put on the train, they could be in that camp right now, sitting around the fire telling stories and eating good potato soup.

AVRAM: There's no fire. There are no stories. There's no potato soup, good or otherwise. Believe me, we're the smart ones. We've still got a gun.

NETTI: So we'll make a meal of the gun, then. The only real question is what will kill us first, starvation or the Germans?

AVRAM: I think the Germans are a good bet, actually. *(He reaches out to touch her.)* We chose the best of the evils. At least we're not alone at the end.

NETTI: Some choice, really. Would we be here still together if it wasn't for the war?

AVRAM: We would have worked it out. There's never been a divorce in my family.

NETTI: You love to say that. Well, thank the war then, for keeping the family record intact. Because, believe me, our divorce would have been the first, mister assistant professor.

AVRAM: Show me one Jew at the university who ever made full professor. Are you still berating me for what I am?

NETTI: The Germans are going to kill us. So does it matter? It all dies with us, anyway.

AVRAM: Yes. They'll never know.

NETTI: What?

AVRAM: When they kill me, my theory dies with me.

NETTI: Again.

AVRAM: Yes, again. Eight years of my life.

NETTI: And six years of mine. Enough.

AVRAM: My unified field theory is…

AVRAM AND NETTI TOGETHER: …a monumental breakthrough in physics and mathematics.

NETTI: I know.

AVRAM: For centuries, science has looked for that one physical law which explains everything. The movements of the galaxies, the entire concept of mass…

NETTI: *(Desperately, looking to the heavens.)* If you're going to drop a bomb on this place, do it now.

AVRAM: ...the meaning of light and energy. At long last, the answer has begun to emerge. The first unified field theory. But my notes...gone. When the Germans kill me, the theory will be lost.

NETTI: Your goddamn theory.

AVRAM: Don't take the Lord's name in vain.

NETTI: Don't you understand that it's your obsession with the goddamn theory...

AVRAM: Please don't take the Lord's...

NETTI: All right, all right. It's all you ever talked about, all you ever thought about. The theory. Maddening, absolutely maddening. Now the Germans are going to kill us...*kill us*...and you're still jabbering about the theory.

AVRAM : They'll succeed in destroying the last Jew in the ghetto, but it will cost science the explanation of how the entire universe functions.

NETTI: The entire universe, is it? Beyond Krakow, even. To the North Pole. To the North Star.

AVRAM: Farther. To the limits of space, and of time, as well. To the creation of physical order. To the absolute meaning of infinity. To the very beginnings of being.

NETTI: Imagine that.

AVRAM: A monumental loss. God will punish them.

NETTI: *(Moving away from him, to the window.)* And how do you think God will pay them back for killing me? I'm not as monumental a loss as you, so I imagine the punishment will not be nearly so severe.

AVRAM: I've always loved you, Netti, no matter what you think. Doesn't that count for anything? You're distorting my meaning.

NETTI: Talk about distortion. Your sense of what is happening here is quite strange.

AVRAM: The significance is very clear to me. My theory could tie together everything man has tried to learn about the cosmos for a thousand years. I am an opportunity which has somehow appeared in the continuum of collective intelligence, only to be destroyed by wild animals. It's a tragedy for me to die without imparting what I know to another person. The cost to science is staggering.

NETTI: And what am I, a bowl of borscht? What's my life worth? When they kill you it's a catastrophe, and when they kill me, it's what…kind of a prank, right?

AVRAM: I never said that. I would never say such a thing.

NETTI: The Germans are all around us. There's no food. We are one hundred percent certain we're going to die. And all you can think about is your goddamn theory.

AVRAM: I said, don't take the Lord's…

NETTI: What am I to you, after all? All right, I'm not some grand theory, only a woman. But there are plenty of people who think I bring a measure of beauty into this life. I'll be missed, you can be sure. Not by you, but by…

AVRAM: I'll be dead, too. *(He goes to her. Tenderly.)* But if I were alive, I would miss you. Terribly.

NETTI: I can't believe it.

AVRAM: Yes, really I would. Why would I say such a…

NETTI: No, I mean I can't believe what I see down there. Somebody's actually walking right down the middle of the street, coming this way. Look.

AVRAM: Where? It's getting dark, hard to see.

NETTI: There. In the second block. Where the dairy store used to be. See?

AVRAM: No, I…Yes, now I see something. What is it?

NETTI: A man.

AVRAM: What's he carrying? Looks like a flag of some sort.

NETTI: Yes, it's a flag.

AVRAM: Is it a soldier? Could he possibly be carrying a flag of truce? It couldn't be surrender. Is this meant for us? I can't believe they'd want to talk to us, in any case.

NETTI: Isn't a flag of truce supposed to be white? The flag isn't white. It's checkered.

AVRAM: A checkered flag? What is this, a war or an automobile race?

NETTI: He's dressed all in white. Big white hat, too. And what's that he's carrying, a suitcase?

AVRAM: A basket of some sort. *(Pulling NETTI away from the window.)* He's looking up. He'll see us.

NETTI: *(Peeking out the window.)* He has seen us. He's waving.

AVRAM: Waving! The bloody arrogance. Ah well, they know where we are now. It won't be long.

NETTI: He's headed right for this building.

AVRAM: *(Picking up his rifle.)* Coming in here to finish us off. He'll have a fight on his hands.

NETTI: One person? Why would the Germans send one person to get us? Why not send a battalion?

AVRAM: It's a trick.

NETTI: Strange trick. He's coming into the building. He's still waving. Now he's smiling.

AVRAM: Smiling, indeed. I'll get him as soon as he walks through the door. *(He pauses to listen.)* I hear him on the stairs.

NETTI: Wait. We ought to see what…

AVRAM: We'll take no chances. As soon as I see him…

> *AVRAM trains his rifle on the door. There is a long silence. Then there is a knock, and JEAN-PAUL opens the door. He wears white chef's garb, including a tall white chef's toque. He sees the gun pointed at him, screams in fright and slams the door.*

NETTI: Something tells me he's not a Nazi soldier.

JEAN-PAUL: *(From outside the door.)* Wait! Wait!

NETTI: Who are you? What do you want?

JEAN-PAUL: Don't shoot me. You don't understand. I'm not here to harm you. *(He opens the door a few inches, pokes his "flag" inside and waves it vigorously. The "flag" is a checkered dinner napkin tied to a tree branch.)*

AVRAM: Who are you? You'd better speak up. We're going to start shooting.

JEAN-PAUL: No, wait! I am chef Jean-Paul, of the Cafe Maddalena.

AVRAM: A chef? From some restaurant?

JEAN-PAUL: *(Affronted.)* Some restaurant? The Cafe Maddalena, only the finest eating establishment in the city, if not the entire region.

NETTI: What do you want with us? Why are you here?

JEAN-PAUL: *(He withdraws the "flag." from the door opening. Very slowly, he swings the door open and steps into the room, holding a large picnic basket before him.)* I have brought your dinner.

AVRAM: *(Incredulously.)* Our what?

JEAN-PAUL: Dinner.

NETTI: Dinner?

JEAN-PAUL: Yes.

AVRAM: You've brought dinner?

JEAN-PAUL: Dinner, dinner. The meal that comes after lunch.

NETTI: Food? For us?

JEAN-PAUL: And what food! Believe me, no one ever had a last meal like this. Not even Marie Antoinette, before they…*(He makes a chopping motion on the back of his neck.)* This meal is a remarkable accomplishment, given the war, the scarcity of quality ingredients. Would you believe, I am actually reduced to substituting carp fillets in my Sole a la Piemontaise. *(He sets down the basket, opens it, and removes a checkered tablecloth which matches the napkin on his "flag." He puts the tablecloth on a small table, then busies himself setting the table meticulously as he talks with AVRAM and NETTI. From the basket, he removes candleholders, then candles which he puts in the holders. Then, also from the basket, he adds napkins, china, silver and glassware.)* But no vulgar substitutions for you. Everything is authentic. Everything. For you, it will be one gustatory tingle after another, until you are…

AVRAM: Do you mean to tell us that you've come here to serve us a fancy dinner?

JEAN-PAUL: Dinner. Is this such a difficult concept to grasp? I've gone to an immoderate amount of trouble.

NETTI: It's simply that it's hard for us to believe you've made your way through this…this battlefield, just to bring us a meal. Why would you do such a thing?

JEAN-PAUL: Why not? *(He removes a bottle of wine from the basket and begins to open it.)* A Montrachet to go with the hors d'oeuvres. Assertive, but not presumptuous.

NETTI: You haven't answered the question. Why have you carried this huge basket of food through the streets? The Germans are trying very hard to kill us, you know.

JEAN-PAUL: Yes, I know. We know.

NETTI: We?

JEAN-PAUL: Not everyone is trying to kill you. The Germans, yes. But some of us…more than you might think…are saddened by the fate that awaits you. And we applaud your courage. Of course there's no way we can save you, but…we wanted to provide you some pleasure for your last hours.

AVRAM: I don't believe it.

JEAN-PAUL: Why is that? Do you think the whole world has been marshaled against you? Just because the Germans want you dead, don't conclude that everyone is on their side.

AVRAM: So you risk your life to bring us food. If the Germans catch you…*(He sees JEAN-PAUL strike a match to light the candles.)* Don't do that. They'll see the light.

JEAN-PAUL: *(Lighting the candles.)* Oh, the Germans know I'm here.

NETTI: They do?

JEAN-PAUL: Certainly. How could I have made my way here without permission? There are soldiers surrounding this sector.

AVRAM: They know where we are, Netti and I?

JEAN-PAUL: Of course.

AVRAM: Then why don't they finish us off. As they want us dead so badly, why would they let you bring us food?

JEAN-PAUL: Because I prevailed upon the commander, Major Werner, to allow you one final, exquisite meal before the bombardment.

AVRAM: Why would he agree to that?

JEAN-PAUL: Most nights Major Werner takes his dinner at Cafe Maddalena. I make him schnitzels. Do you know what a schnitzel is? A cutlet breaded and fried. Typical German fare, impossibly heavy and greasy, perfectly suited to the digestive process of a Nazi. Major Werner is devoted to my schnitzels, and therefore much beholden to me. So when I asked him this favor, he could scarcely refuse me. When you think about it, what difference does it make to him, really? He can kill you now or after you've eaten. *(He has finished setting the table, and now he pours wine into two glasses from the table.)* If you'll put down your gun and take your wine, I'll serve the hors d'oeuvres.

AVRAM: Just a minute. Not so quickly. The wine is good, eh?

JEAN-PAUL: A Montrachet. You'll like it.

AVRAM: Then you won't mind having a bit of it yourself.

NETTI: Avram…

AVRAM: This is all such a crazy story. Who knows what's in that bottle. *(To JEAN-PAUL.)* Go ahead.

JEAN-PAUL: Certainly. *(He takes a glass from the basket and pours a bit of the wine into it. He holds the glass up to the light, swirls the wine around in the glass, then carefully smells the aroma of the wine. Then he takes a sip, retains the wine in his mouth for a moment, and finally swallows it. AVRAM and NETTI watch his every move intently. He looks at them thoughtfully, and smiles.)* An amusing little wine. *(He sets down his own glass, then picks up the two glasses he has poured for AVRAM and NETTI. NETTI accepts the wine, but AVRAM does not. JEAN-PAUL reaches into the basket and takes out a plate filled with hors d'oeuvres)* Anchovies a la Russe and Mushroom Croquettes with a touch of Madiera Sauce. *(He holds the plate out to them, but they hesitate. He realizes that they are still suspicious of what he has brought.)* Ah, yes. *(He takes an hors d'oeuvre and eats it. NETTI quickly reaches for one, but stops because she sees that AVRAM continues to hesitate.)* Well? What's the trouble now?

AVRAM: Is it kosher?

JEAN-PAUL: Kosher? Kosher!

AVRAM: Yes, was this food prepared in a kosher kitchen? The pots…the plates?

NETTI: How can you possibly…

JEAN-PAUL: My dear sir, the world has gone utterly mad. Everywhere, people are destroying each other for reasons that make no sense, and at a pace which is truly horrifying. Wherever one looks, there is misery and grief beyond description. People are unbearably hungry, in pain, past all hope of saving their lives, or even their souls. All around, there is sorrow and heartache. You yourself are trapped in the rubble of a ravaged community, waiting to be blown to shreds by a Nazi bombardment, this lovely lady with you, sharing your devastation. With immense difficulty, I have managed to transcend these barbaric conditions and create what is surely the last civilized meal you will ever taste in this world. AND YOU ARE ASKING IF THIS FOOD IS KOSHER!

AVRAM: I eat only kosher food.

NETTI: For God's sake, at a time like this...

AVRAM: Yes, for God's sake, indeed. Our religion says we are to eat only kosher food.

NETTI: Isn't this an exception? Isn't this an extraordinary circumstance?

AVRAM: The rules haven't changed just because we're hungry. If God wants us to...

NETTI: Who are you to say what God wants? I'm sure God has a great deal more sense than you do. Do you really think God puts us here in the ghetto to give our lives fighting the Nazis, pushes us to the limits of our endurance, starves us for days until we're so weak we can barely stand, sends this fellow in here with a wonderful meal...and then has the chutzpah to tell us, "Don't eat it, it's not kosher?" What kind of a God is that?

AVRAM: A God who is testing us.

NETTI: Testing? You think God has brought all of this about to test us?

AVRAM: Yes.

NETTI: Then I fail. (*With both hands, she begins taking hors d'oeuvres from the plate and eating them.*)

JEAN-PAUL: She's right, you know. You've given so much, and you're ready to sacrifice everything that remains. Would God deprive you of a bite to eat? I assure you, I am not the devil, here to tempt you.

NETTI: *(Continuing to eat, pausing briefly only to wash the food down with wine.)* I don't know which kind is better. They're both so delicious. Avram, I insist you eat this marvelous food. Go on. Would God ask you to starve to death? *(She holds an hors d'oeuvre up to his mouth, but still he hesitates.)* No? All right, then. *(She puts it into her own mouth.)*

JEAN-PAUL: Don't be foolish. God wants you to live as long as you can. Eat.

> *AVRAM stares in silence at the plate of food. NETTI and JEAN-PAUL watch as he slowly takes an hors d'oeuvre in his hand, turns it to inspect it from every possible angle, nibbles a tiny piece of it, then finally puts it into his mouth.*

JEAN-PAUL: What do you think?

> *AVRAM nods his head and takes two more hors d'oeuvres, one in each hand. NETTI takes those remaining, and the plate is empty.*

JEAN-PAUL: Wise choice. Live every moment, I say. Well, now, since this is settled, we can move on to the salad course. Please take your seats.

NETTI: This is a dream. A wonderful dream that is somehow taking place in the middle of a nightmare.

> *NETTI and AVRAM find chairs and pull them up to the table. JEAN-PAUL begins serving from the basket.*

JEAN-PAUL: This is a creation of my own, and a favorite at Cafe Maddalena. I call it Salade Demi-Deuil. Not terribly difficult to execute, once you know where you're going. The real glory is in the concept. Basically, it's equal parts artichoke bottoms and truffles, cut in julienne and seasoned with mustard and cream. You will find it entices the palate, preparing the taste buds for the meal that is to come.

NETTI: Wonderful. I've never eaten anything remotely like it. Truffles, you say?

JEAN-PAUL: Yes, they impart a certain ah, ah…je ne sais quoi. How does one describe the taste of a truffle? *(To AVRAM.)* And you, sir? What is your verdict on the salad?

AVRAM: It's very good. I never tasted a truffle before.

JEAN-PAUL: Really? Never?

AVRAM: Jews don't eat truffles.

JEAN-PAUL: Oh, come, now.

AVRAM: No, it's true. I never knew a Jew who ate a truffle. I never knew a Jew who could afford a truffle.

JEAN-PAUL: You must travel in a limited circle of Jews.

AVRAM: Academics. Intellectuals. We'd rather argue about philosophy than enjoy fine food. We didn't have the money to eat like gourmets, anyway.

JEAN-PAUL: Pity.

AVRAM: I wasn't brought up with fancy food. Some black bread. A bowl of barley soup. Some roasted brisket. Maybe on the sabbath a cholent. That was it.

JEAN-PAUL: What is a cholent?

AVRAM: Beans and meat and…*(Looking to NETTI.)* Well, like a stew, yes…?

NETTI: A cholent is beans and onions and pieces of potato and some good, fat meat, all in a big pot. It goes into the oven before sundown on Friday night, before the sabbath starts…

AVRAM: A Jew mustn't light the oven once the sabbath has begun.

NETTI: The cholent cooks slowly through the night on Friday, and all Saturday morning. After services on Saturday, we eat the cholent.

AVRAM: By that time, the most irresistible aroma has filled every room in the house, and the beans on the top of the cholent have become brown and crispy. I used to fight with my brothers to get the crispy beans when we sat down to eat on Saturday. Mmmm, delicious. A taam ganaiden. *(Pronounced TAHM gahn-AYDEN.)*

JEAN-PAUL: What?

NETTI: A taste of paradise.

JEAN-PAUL: Sounds a bit like a cassoulet. Does it have confit of duck?

AVRAM: What's that?

JEAN-PAUL: Pieces of cooked duck preserved in duck fat.

AVRAM: No, never heard of it.

JEAN-PAUL: Or pork sausages?

AVRAM: Not in my neighborhood.

JEAN-PAUL: Had I known you were so fond of bean dishes, I'd have made you a cassoulet. Maybe next time.

NETTI: *(Wistfully.)* Yes, next time.

JEAN-PAUL: Sorry. Just a figure of speech. Thoughtless of me.

NETTI: No, no. We understand.

JEAN-PAUL: In any case, let us move on, for I wasn't given much time, and the best is to come. *(He clears the salad plates.)* It's gauche, I know, but we'll have to re-use the wine glasses. I ran out of room. Please finish the white, and we'll open the red. *(He opens the new bottle as they finish the white wine in their glasses, and pours it.)* I shouldn't be surprised if this were the last bottle of Chambertin left in the city. The Germans drank up all the burgundies first. Can you imagine a steady diet of the great wines? And with schnitzels! It's too much. Staggers the senses. The legendary burgundies, they're all gone. Clos-Vougeot. Musigny. Pomard. Romanee. Even Volnay. Probably won't see them again until after the war. If it ever ends. Let's see, now. Ah, yes, Potatoes a la Paysanne. (*He begins serving food from covered pans and dishes which he takes from the basket.*)

AVRAM: You've done something fancy with potatoes?

JEAN-PAUL: "Fancy" is hardly adequate. "Extraordinary" is more appropriate. Very thin round slices of potato alternated with chopped sorrel which has been cooked briefly in butter. Pounded chervil and a bit of minced garlic mixed in. Then some stock, and salt and pepper. A few more dabs of butter on top, and it all goes into the oven until the potatoes soften, the flavors mature and the top browns. It's still quite hot.

NETTI: It smells wonderful.

JEAN-PAUL: Some young glazed carrots, as much for color as for flavor. And finally, my gustatory triumph, the signature dish of Cafe Maddalena. People came from everywhere for a taste of this. Chausson de Jambon au Fois Gras. Behold. An oval of pastry is covered with a layer of foie gras, tossed in butter, upon which the slices of meat are placed. Then more foie gras, and finally a top layer of pastry, which is sealed against the bottom layer. We glaze with a wash of beaten egg, poke holes to let the steam escape and bake in a very hot oven. Then we serve it with a touch of Port Sauce, like this.

NETTI: I've never seen food like this in my life. Not even at weddings. (*Tasting.*) Oh, this is extraordinary. This is a whole new world of sensations. It's far beyond anything I've ever tasted. What a revelation!

> AVRAM *does not respond, or even look up from his plate. He eats ravenously, and continuously.*

JEAN-PAUL: I'm so pleased to be able to introduce you one of life's great pleasures. One should be able to sample all the good things this mortal existence of ours has to offer, even if...even if...

NETTI: Even if the end is near.

JEAN-PAUL: Yes, I suppose so.

NETTI: I agree. After all, why have we been given senses if we don't use them? And why appetites if we don't appease them? Oh, these potatoes are heavenly.

JEAN-PAUL: Thank you. Without question, there is a divine plan that tells us to live and be happy. And that is my calling, to bring people pleasure. I'm convinced of it. Do you want to hear how I know this?

NETTI: Yes. How do you know?

JEAN-PAUL: I was one of nine children, the son of a working man who was so poor he couldn't buy enough food to feed his family. One day, in desperation, he gave me the few coins he had in his pocket and abandoned me. He told me I had to make my own way, to find a door that would open to me. Then he vanished. I was thirteen years old. I wandered through the city for days, hungry and frantic. In the end, destiny led me to a small restaurant, where the owner put me to work in the kitchen, and let me sleep in an attic loft after long days among the pots and pans. I might have found my way to the shop of a carpenter or a locksmith or a tailor. But no. A divine hand pointed me to a kitchen, where my gifts soon became apparent. The owner taught me what he knew, and in a few years my own skills surpassed his. The people adored my cooking, and came from all over the city to dine. I was sous chef by the time I was seventeen. At twenty-three, executive chef of the Cafe Maddalena. It was my destiny.

NETTI: You must know everything there is to know about food.

JEAN-PAUL: One never knows everything about food. It's important to know food, of course, but more important to know about people. About life. Because dining is more than tasting. It is a total experience, a convergence where intelligence meets all our senses. *(To AVRAM.)* You are very busy eating, my friend. I take that to mean you like what I've prepared.

AVRAM: *(Still eating.)* Yes, it's really good. Excellent, in fact. The potatoes are very tasty. And the little carrots, I never knew carrots could be so small and so sweet. But best of all is the meat in the pie-crust. *(He takes a piece of meat and chews it enthusiastically.)* It's just wonderful. What did you say it was?

JEAN-PAUL: Chausson de Jambon au Foie Gras. Jambon. Ham.

AVRAM: *(As he hears the word "ham," he coughs violently, spitting out food and clutching at his own throat.)* Ham! Oh my God, ham! I've eaten the meat of a pig!

JEAN-PAUL: I thought we'd gotten past all that.

AVRAM: This is terrible! In my whole life I never put such a thing into my mouth. And now, on my last day on earth, I've eaten ham. Oh, my God, forgive me! Netti, we've eaten ham.

NETTI: *(Eating enthusiastically.)* It's good, too.

AVRAM: No one in my family has ever eaten the meat of a pig. Oh, this is a disgrace. It is absolutely…. *(To NETTI.)* What did you say?

NETTI: I said it's good.

AVRAM: *(Horrified.)* And what makes you think so?

NETTI: I believe it's the sauce.

JEAN-PAUL: I don't understand. We went all through this with the hors d'oeuvres, and you finally decided that, because of the circumstances, you could eat food that wasn't kosher. Now you're so terribly upset because of a piece of ham. What's the difference?

AVRAM: Not kosher is one thing. Ham is something else again. Anything that comes from a pig is unclean…absolutely forbidden.

JEAN-PAUL: So you're telling me there's forbidden and then there's absolutely forbidden. It's worse to eat ham than, say, non-kosher beef?

NETTI: Well, it depends what part of the steer the beef came from.

JEAN-PAUL: Oh, come, now.

NETTI: No, really. We're not supposed to eat any cut of beef that comes from the animal's hindquarters.

AVRAM: We're not talking about beef. You fed us ham. You should have known. You knew we were Jews, didn't you?

JEAN-PAUL: Yes, but…Look, many prosperous Jews would come to Cafe Maddalena to dine, before the war. They ate everything that was on the menu. Pork, beef, lobsters, anything. Why was it all right for them, but not for you?

AVRAM: I'll tell you why. Because those people were not real Jews. They were reformed Jews.

JEAN PAUL: Oh? And what are reformed Jews if they're not Jews?

AVRAM: We always thought of them as gentiles.

JEAN-PAUL: I'm afraid these distinctions escape me. Oh, dear. I've tried so hard to do something good here, and I've made a mess of it.

NETTI: *(Getting up and going to JEAN-PAUL.)* No, no, no, no. You've done a wonderful thing here. A beautiful and selfless gesture. An incredible meal. Better than incredible. Brilliant. *(Indicating*

AVRAM.) He's the one who's making a mess of it all. All this talk about kosher, and forbidden. Who cares any more? Not me.

AVRAM: Be careful. God is listening.

NETTI: Are you certain?

AVRAM: He hears every word that comes out of your mouth.

NETTI: Well, then, if He's paying attention, this might be a good time to speak what's on my mind. I have a few thoughts I would like to express.

AVRAM: Be careful, now. God does not take kindly to rudeness.

NETTI: God told you this? He descended from the cosmos to whisper in your ear? He said to you, "Avram, I put up with a lot of stupid notions, but there are two things I just won't tolerate. Ham is one and rudeness is the other." *(Loosening up.)* I had some white wine, and I had some red wine. And now it's all becoming quite clear to me.

JEAN-PAUL: What's becoming so clear?

NETTI: Everything. The object of it all. He thinks he has it all figured out with a special theory of his...

AVRAM: My unified field theory.

NETTI: His unified field theory. It explains everything...why the sun comes up in the morning and the stars drift across the sky at night. But what it does not do, this theory of his, is tell us why we're having our last meal, why we're preparing ourselves to die. I'll have some more of the red, please.

JEAN-PAUL pours more wine into NETTI's glass.

AVRAM: Because the Nazis have sworn to...

NETTI: Please. I'm talking to God. I'm not such a great intellect that I can begin to understand the grand movements of history, the wars and the plagues and the persecutions that You allow to happen. I must admit, they look like rather bad judgment on Your part, but I accept that You must have Your reasons. No, it's the small matters that concern me, the things I can grasp. We resolved that we would never go to the camps, that we would die in the ghetto fighting the Nazis. The ghetto is Jewish, and if they wanted to take it, we would make them pay for it. Until the end. We would become, not Jewish victims, but Jewish heroes. *(She takes a sip of wine.)* I'm beginning to think this was not such a shrewd idea.

AVRAM: Are you questioning the…

NETTI: Yes. I'm asking why we all chose between two paths, both of which lead to our deaths. Because I don't think that was what He had in mind.

AVRAM: Who's second-guessing the Almighty now?

NETTI: Listen, God, we hadn't had a morsel of food in days, so what did You do? You sent this lovely man to bring the best meal we ever ate. To me, that's not a sign You want us to die. So it's not kosher. Where were You going to find a kosher kitchen with a war on? We understand. The big picture here is that You sent food when we were hungry. We know what that means! You want us to live! *(She drains the rest of the wine in her glass.)* Am I right?

JEAN-PAUL: It makes a great deal of sense.

AVRAM: Right or wrong, what difference does it make? We picked our path, and this is it. They know where we are, the Germans, and they're going to destroy us. We can't simply choose to live. They're not going to let us. One way or another, they'll kill all the Jews.

JEAN-PAUL: Don't you want to live?

AVRAM: I'm not afraid to die.

NETTI: That's not the point. So you're brave. You were always brave. But why are you so determined to achieve this grim fate? You don't have to prove yourself by giving up your life.

AVRAM: I'm determined to fight to the end.

NETTI: God does not want you to die.

AVRAM: So why did He send me ham? Why didn't He send me a tank?

NETTI: Some things you have to do for yourself. I don't want to die, and Avram, I don't want you to die. I care for you. This battle in the ghetto is over. There's nothing we can gain by fighting, not anymore. The only way our lives can mean anything now is for us to refuse to die, to show them we insist on living in spite of them.

JEAN-PAUL: May I serve you some more before it grows cold?

AVRAM: Just the potatoes and the carrots, please.

JEAN-PAUL: *(Sadly.)* No more Chausson de Jambon, then?

NETTI: I'll have his. And more wine, too.

AVRAM: *(To NETTI.)* Enjoy it, then. There's nothing we can do. Just remember, whatever happens now, that you are my own true love, and always have been.

NETTI: Avram, you see into the mysteries of the universe. Smart you are, but I'm not sure if you're wise.

AVRAM: No? Maybe not. What should a wise man do now? Make a miracle?

NETTI: Yes, you're smart. Make a miracle. Didn't you always tell me that no problem is too difficult if you focus on it with all your energy.

AVRAM: There's nothing we can do, believe me.

NETTI: Nothing. *(A pause.)* Then you are simply willing to let the Nazis deprive the world of your unified field theory.

AVRAM: A tragedy.

NETTI: *(Quickly agreeing with him.)* A terrible loss. It will set science back a hundred years.

AVRAM: *(His enthusiasm growing.)* It explains the spectrum shifts in the stars, you know.

NETTI: No one must be permitted to destroy it.

AVRAM: It's the first theory that clarifies why mass changes with velocity. It's a breakthrough in the mathematics of physics.

NETTI: Your unified field theory must survive, at any cost.

AVRAM: The ramifications in astrophysics alone are immense.

NETTI: *(Seing that AVRAM is responding to her arguments, NETTI gestures to JEAN-PAUL, encouraging him to join in.)* We must succeed in safeguarding the theory. We owe it to mankind.

JEAN-PAUL: Er...yes. Your theory is...ah...absolutely vital. Without question, you must save yourselves...ah...so the theory will survive.

AVRAM: Yes!

NETTI: Wise choice.

AVRAM: But how? There are thousands of Germans, all around us.

JEAN-PAUL: Well, no, not thousands. I don't think. Not any more. Wait until you taste this dessert.

NETTI: But there were thousands.

JEAN-PAUL: Yes, but that's when there were thousands of you, too. By today there were only a handful of Jews left. Now there's just you. Major Werner wouldn't keep so many troops here just to defeat two people.

NETTI: So how many are there?

JEAN-PAUL: I saw maybe fifty or so. All around these few blocks. This is chestnut pudding. A sweet celebration, if I may say. We cook the chestnuts in a light vanilla-flavored syrup, then puree them before adding them to an egg custard. To finish, apricot sauce, flavored with kirsch. And, oh yes, some petits fours for you to nibble on. Go ahead.

NETTI: *(Eating her pudding.)* Fifty soldiers can't cover every square foot. It's dark now. Maybe we can slip away. *(To JEAN-PAUL.)* Delicious.

JEAN-PAUL: Thank you.

AVRAM: *(Eating his pudding.)* Really very good. You know, I could get used to food like this. Fifty of them, and two of us with a single rifle. The odds are awful. Impossible.

JEAN-PAUL: And what were the odds that a 13-year-old boy would find his way to a restaurant, and become a great chef?

NETTI: Yes. Just think of that.

JEAN-PAUL: In any case, the imperative is the same, isn't it?

AVRAM: The imperative?

JEAN-PAUL: Live. That's the imperative. The critical thing.

NETTI: The only thing. You know, I remember seeing a sewer grating in the alley behind this building. Is it possible that we might get into the sewer and make our way out of the ghetto right under their feet?

AVRAM: Too obvious. I can't believe others haven't tried it.

NETTI: Still.

AVRAM: And even if we do get beyond the ghetto, we'll have hundreds of miles to go to safe haven…miles filled with God-knows-how-many soldiers.

NETTI: Still.

AVRAM: Still, we're going to try, aren't we?

JEAN-PAUL: What can you lose?

NETTI: Will he make trouble for you, this Major Werner, if we overcome the odds and get away?

JEAN-PAUL: I'll tell him I tried to stop you, but you ran out the door. What can he do? No Jean-Paul, no schnitzels.

AVRAM: If we're going to do it, let's go now.

NETTI: Yes, now. Now or never.

> *NETTI and AVRAM get up from the table. AVRAM picks up his rifle.*

NETTI: *(Hugging JEAN-PAUL.)* Goodbye. Thank you for the dinner. Thank you for everything.

AVRAM: How can I begin to thank you. Goodbye, until we meet again.

JEAN-PAUL: Next time I'll make you a cholent. Goodbye, and good luck.

JEAN-PAUL: *(He watches after NETTI and AVRAM as they leave, then looks back to the table.)* They never tasted my petits fours.

> *NETTI hurries back in through the door, goes to the table and scoops up the petits fours. She smiles at JEAN-PAUL and hurries back out the door.*

JEAN-PAUL: Yes. Live.

> *The lights fade to black.*

THE LAST REQUEST
OF EDDIE
CARMICHAEL/COHEN

THE CHARACTERS

Carmichael/Cohen, a sick man in his 70s

Sister Veronica, a nun

Rabbi Murray Schecter

Esther Goldman, a woman in her 60s

THE PLACE

A hospital room

THE TIME

Now

CARMICHAEL/COHEN lies on his bed, which is cranked up to near-sitting position. He is clearly quite sick, with an I.V. tube in the back of his hand, and another tube in his nose. There is an untouched tray of food, and a vase of flowers.

CARMICHAEL/COHEN: *(There is no one else in the room, yet he addresses an imaginary listener. He speaks with some effort, gasping for breath.)* So don't get so high and mighty with me, my friend. You think you're my better, do you? Did you know that my family was Viennese aristocracy? Before the war my parents were the most respected Jews in Austria, next to the Rothschilds. Oh, and maybe Sigmund Freud. He was Jewish, you know. So was his cigar. Jewish, I mean. Jewish cigar. *(He laughs.)* You know what he said? He said, "Sometimes a cigar is just a cigar." He was trying to make it clear, the difference between a cigar and a penis…what a man smokes and what he diddles with. *(SISTER VERONICA enters the room and stands watching him, though he does not address her.)* Hi diddle diddle, the cat and the fiddle. Is it the truth, or is it a riddle? *(Noticing SISTER VERONICA. Annoyed.)* What?

SISTER VERONICA: Did you eat your lunch? Are you finished?

CARMICHAEL/COHEN: No, I didn't get lunch.

SISTER VERONICA: There it is, right there.

CARMICHAEL/COHEN: That is not lunch.

SISTER VERONICA: What is it, then?

CARMICHAEL/COHEN: Well, it's not lunch. Lunch is supposed to be food. The stuff on this tray does not fall into that category.

SISTER VERONICA: It's light, easily digestible food. It's what the doctor says you can have.

CARMICHAEL/COHEN: That sanctimonious old fart.

SISTER VERONICA: Please.

CARMICHAEL/COHEN : He doesn't have enough sense to feed a dying man whatever he wants. I'm on my way out. What difference does it make what I eat? Would you look at this broth. My urine bottle looks tastier than this. And this pudding. It's a dish full of brown slime. You're trying to hasten my death, you and that fat-ass doctor. It's a conspiracy against the Jews, that's what it is.

SISTER VERONICA: There's no conspiracy, and you stop that talk about being Jewish. You're a good Catholic man, and you know it.

CARMICHAEL/COHEN: That's what you think, Sister Smarty Pants. You're not aware of my background. My family was Hungarian aristocracy. Rich Jews, respected in Buda and in Pest—both sides of the Moldau.

SISTER VERONICA: I believe it's the Danube River that flows through Budapest.

CARMICHAEL/COHEN: *(Dismissing her comment with a wave of his hand.)* My grandfather David had a shoe factory, it took up a whole city block. It was him who invented saddle shoes, you know that?

SISTER VERONICA: Oh, please...

CARMICHAEL/COHEN: God's truth. Before the war, everybody in Hungary was wearing his saddle shoes. Not like today, black and white or brown and white. In those days, they were green and white. Grandpa David's idea.

SISTER VERONICA: We're short-handed today, Mother Evelyn is away, and I really don't have time for this nonsense. I wish you'd eat your lunch.

CARMICHAEL/COHEN: Then get me something decent.

SISTER VERONICA: What is it that you want?

CARMICHAEL/COHEN: Get me a hot pastrami on rye, and a bottle of celery tonic. A sour pickle would be nice, too.

SISTER VERONICA: There's no way I can get those things, and you can't have them anyway. Spicy food will just make you sick.

CARMICHAEL/COHEN: That's a laugh. Sicker than I am, you mean?

SISTER VERONICA: Be reasonable. You won't even be able to get it down.

CARMICHAEL/COHEN: Just a taste of the pastrami. And you could pour the celery tonic into my I.V. drip.

SISTER VERONICA: Fatty sandwiches and soda. Is that what your family ate in Hungary?

CARMICHAEL/COHEN: Where?

SISTER VERONICA: In Hungary. Where your family came from.

CARMICHAEL/COHEN: Where did you hear that? My family came from England.

SISTER VERONICA: Didn't you just say…

CARMICHAEL/COHEN: They were aristocrats. My Aunt Sophie made the best bagels in London. She had a phenomenal love affair with the Prince of Wales.

SISTER VERONICA: Oh, come now…

CARMICHAEL/COHEN: God's truth. Sophie was the first one to put sesame seeds on bagels. The Prince took one bite and he lost his heart to her. If they had married, Englishmen today would be eating bagels for breakfast instead of kippers.

SISTER VERONICA: Where do you get these outrageous ideas?

CARMICHAEL/COHEN: Are you going to get my pastrami and celery tonic?

SISTER VERONICA: Of course not.

CARMICHAEL/COHEN: Well, then, maybe just the sour pickle?

SISTER VERONICA: No sour pickle, either. Of all things.

CARMICHAEL/COHEN: I knew it. I predicted it. A dying man is at the mercy of his Catholic jailers. Don't think you can trifle with me, Sister Smart-Ass. I come from a family of aristocrats. We were the most respected Jews…

SISTER VERONICA: You are Edward Carmichael of St. Joseph's parish. And while I cannot make you eat, I believe you'll feel better if you have your lunch.

CARMICHAEL/COHEN: How would you know?

> *RABBI SCHECTER enters. He wears a solemn dark suit and a black fedora hat.*

RABBI SCHECTER: Excuse me, is this the room of Eddie Cohen?

SISTER VERONICA: No, I'm afraid not. You have the wrong room.

RABBI SCHECTER: *(Turning to leave.)* Sorry.

CARMICHAEL/COHEN: You're in the right place, rabbi.

SISTER VERONICA: What?

CARMICHAEL/COHEN: This is it. The room of Eddie Cohen.

SISTER VERONICA: It is not.

CARMICHAEL/COHEN: *(To SISTER VERONICA.)* Would you stop arguing with everything I say. *(To RABBI SCHECTER.)* Rabbi… what is it again?

RABBI SCHECTER: Schecter. I am Rabbi Murray Schecter.

CARMICHAEL/COHEN: I'm Eddie Cohen, Rabbi Schectman. I'm the one who phoned you.

SISTER VERONICA: You called this man to come here? Why would you do that?

RABBI SCHECTER: You said it was critical…life and death.

CARMICHAEL/COHEN: It is. Believe me.

SISTER VERONICA: I apologize for whatever this man has said to you. The truth is, he really shouldn't be…

CARMICHAEL/COHEN: This woman will tell you the most scandalous lies about me, Rabbi Scheer. I'm being held here against my will. God's truth.

SISTER VERONICA: There are things you should know, rabbi. Please come outside a moment.

CARMICHAEL/COHEN: *(Highly irritated.)* Oh, no you don't! No whispered secrets. No intrigues. You Catholics love that stuff, don't you.

SISTER VERONICA: Now, Mr. Carmichael, don't upset yourself. There are merely a few things I must discuss…

RABBI SCHECTER: Carmichael? I thought he was Eddie Cohen.

SISTER VERONICA: That's what I have to talk to you about. You see, he's…

CARMICHAEL/COHEN: *(Ferocious.)* Take Rabbi Schleffler out there to poison his mind against me, and I will rip these tubes out of my body, make my way into the corridor, and die a hideous death on the floor in front of everybody, gasping for breath and cursing the Catholic church. *(He pulls back his blanket and puts one foot onto the floor.)*

How would you like that, Sister Executioner? The high profile death of your patient, on your watch.

SISTER VERONICA: What do you want?

CARMICHAEL/COHEN: He didn't come to talk to you. I'm the one who called him. You want to talk to him, talk to him right here. Where I can listen. This is about me.

SISTER VERONICA: Very well, then. Get back in your bed. Please.

CARMICHAEL/COHEN: *(He does.)* All right. But one thing, before you get started.

SISTER VERONICA: Yes.

CARMICHAEL/COHEN: Not you. Rabbi Schlurman.

RABBI SCHECTER: That's Schecter. Rabbi Murray Schecter.

CARMICHAEL/COHEN: That's what I said. Let me ask you this question, Rabbi...whatever...

RABBI SCHECTER: Yes? What is it?

CARMICHAEL/COHEN: *(After a pause.)* Did you bring me the food item we discussed?

RABBI SCHECTER: No, I did not.

CARMICHAEL/COHEN: Why not?

RABBI SCHECTER: I'm a rabbi, not a delivery boy from the delicatessen.

CARMICHAEL/COHEN: No pastrami?

RABBI SCHECTER: No pastrami.

CARMICHAEL/COHEN: In Our Lady of Mercy Hospital, you were my last hope.

RABBI SCHECTER: Is this what 'life and death' means to you…pastrami?

CARMICHAEL/COHEN: No, no, not at all. Not the main thing. I just thought to myself, what should a dying Jew want for his last meal, and I came up with pastrami. And then I figured, as long as you were on your way…

SISTER VERONICA: Mr. Carmichael has some strange notions, rabbi. He's on a lot of medication, and he's not quite based in reality some of the time…

CARMICHAEL/COHEN: Hi diddle diddle, the cat and the fiddle. They give you a bottle, and you gotta piddle.

SISTER VERONICA: …most of the time, actually.

RABBI SCHECTER: What's wrong with him?

SISTER VERONICA: Well, I don't think I should…

CARMICHAEL/COHEN: Go ahead. Tell him. My life, what's left of it, is an open book.

SISTER VERONICA: Mr. Carmichael is being treated for cancer of the pancreas.

CARMICHAEL/COHEN: Sure, pancreas. That's where it started. Now it's galloping all over. My stomach, my nasal passages, my Eustachian tube. I can feel it moving. There it goes. It's turning down. Whoops! Right to my testicles.

SISTER VERONICA: No such thing.

CARMICHAEL/COHEN: *(Pulling back the covers.)* You want to see?

SISTER VERONICA: *(Pulling up the covers.)* We do not. *(To RABBI SCHECTER.)* He loves to tell everyone he's at death's door. The truth is, he's seriously sick, but he is not in extremis.

CARMICHAEL/COHEN: The truth is, I am in extremis. Do I look like a healthy man to you, Rabbi Solomon? Look how pale and drawn I am. I have no strength. I tremble constantly. The truth is, the angel of death is coming for me tonight, early evening. Right after Jeopardy.

SISTER VERONICA: You're quite sure of that?

CARMICHAEL/COHEN: That's what he told me.

SISTER VERONICA: Oh? When?

CARMICHAEL/COHEN: A minute ago. You saw him. Long hair. Tweed sport jacket.

SISTER VERONICA: He must have slipped by me. He said tonight's the night, then?

CARMICHAEL/COHEN: He said get ready. Whatever you've got to do, get it done before seven-thirty. When they give the answer to final Jeopardy, you're on your way.

RABBI SCHECTER: Look, this is a particularly busy day for me. Why did you choose me to call?

CARMICHAEL/COHEN: Your synagogue is the first one listed in the yellow pages. Starts with a B. Beth…what is it?

RABBI SCHECTER: Beth Hamedresh Hagodel.

CARMICHAEL/COHEN: That's it. And I got lucky. You answered the phone.

RABBI SCHECTER: We're a very small congregation. We don't employ a secretary. Look, Mr. Carmichael…

CARMICHAEL/COHEN: Cohen.

RABBI SCHECTER: All right, then, Mr. Cohen. What do you want of me? How can I help you?

CARMICHAEL/COHEN: I want you to marry me.

RABBI SCHECTER: What!

CARMICHAEL/COHEN: No, poor choice of words. Let me re-phrase that. What I mean to say is, I want you to marry me to a lady…officiate at our wedding. Bless us with the sanctification of the Jewish faith.

SISTER VERONICA: Oh, so now you're getting married.

CARMICHAEL/COHEN: I knew you'd be happy for me.

SISTER VERONICA: Overjoyed. And who is the fortunate woman?

CARMICHAEL/COHEN: You know her. She's been in to see me. Her name is Esther Goldman. Has a lovely ring to it, don't you agree? Esssther Goooldman.

RABBI SCHECTER: Let me see if I understand this. You are either a Catholic named Carmichael, or a Jew named Cohen. The angel of death is coming for you tonight, in either case. And you have called me, Rabbi Schecter…

CARMICHAEL/COHEN: Morris, right?

RABBI SCHECTER: Murray. You have called a rabbi to Our Lady of Mercy Hospital in order to perform a wedding. You wish to be married to some woman…

CARMICHAEL/COHEN: Not 'some woman.' A woman among women. Any man would fall in love with her instantly. I did.

RABBI SCHECTER: And when is this wedding supposed to take place?

CARMICHAEL/COHEN: It has to be today. I told you, by tonight I'll be flying out the window with the angel of death. Goodbye, Eddie Cohen.

SISTER VERONICA: You are nowhere close to the end. Tonight you'll be sound asleep in your bed.

CARMICHAEL/COHEN: There you go again. Everything has to be your way. You insist that I go on living. Don't I ever get to win?

SISTER VERONICA: Where is the bride, then?

CARMICHAEL/COHEN: Esther is on her way. I called her to come. Wait till you meet her.

RABBI SCHECTER: Mr. Carmichael…Cohen…I can't help you.

CARMICHAEL/COHEN: You're a rabbi, aren't you?

RABBI SCHECTER: Yes, of course, but there are…

CARMICHAEL/COHEN: If it's a question of money, I have plenty.

RABBI SCHECTER: Money is not the concern here. In the first place, I can't…won't…consecrate a mixed marriage. I am a conservative Jew, and I can't sanction any marriage where one of the parties is not Jewish.

CARMICHAEL/COHEN: But Esther is Jewish. Esther Goldman.

RABBI SCHECTER: Her, yes. But you?

CARMICHAEL/COHEN: Certainly I am. I told you I was.

RABBI SCHECTER: She says you're not.

CARMICHAEL/COHEN: What does she know? I'm the one who knows whether I'm Jewish or not.

SISTER VERONICA: Mr. Carmichael has been a congregant at St. Joseph's Church for at least thirty years. Father Walsh has been here to visit him half a dozen times. There's no question that his name is Carmichael, and that he is Catholic. You must understand he has these flights of fantasy that…

CARMICHAEL/COHEN: Just give me a chance, will you, Sister Torquemada. I can explain all of this. Will you listen?

SISTER VERONICA: We're listening. Intently.

CARMICHAEL/COHEN: Now, try to follow this. My maternal grandfather was in the court of King Alfonso of Spain when he met my grandmother and fell in love with her. She was the daughter of an aristocratic Jewish family, one of the grandees, as they were called. They married, but she never converted to Catholicism, though they lived as Catholics. They had one daughter, my mother. Now, according to Jews who know, the child takes the religion of the mother. So my mother was Jewish because her mother was Jewish. Right? You with me?

SISTER VERONICA: What about your Hungarian grandfather who invented saddle shoes, and your grandmother who made bagels for the Prince of Wales?

CARMICHAEL/COHEN: What are you talking about? Where does she get these things? Rabbi, listen to me. My mother married Joe Carmichael, an insurance adjuster, in Pittsburgh. But she was never really Catholic, either. So that means…

SISTER VERONICA: Aren't we missing something here? How did this story suddenly move from Spain to America? How did your mother get here?

CARMICHAEL/COHEN: *(Impatient and sarcastic.)* She swam! Is this really important? I'm trying to explain something here, and you're bogging me down with details. The point is, in my genes, and in my heart, I'm a Jew. And according to the rules, I'm a Jew.

SISTER VERONICA: So why have you been going to mass at St. Joseph's for thirty years?

CARMICHAEL/COHEN: I don't know. You get started, you do it a few times, it gets addictive. But now that I'm looking over the precipice, my true faith is calling out to me, And I want to make Esther my wife.

RABBI SCHECTER: You don't need a rabbi to marry you. A justice of the peace can do it. All you need is your marriage license.

CARMICHAEL/COHEN: Got to have a rabbi. I have to validate my Judaism before I leave with the angel. And I don't have a license. That's not the important thing here.

RABBI SCHECTER: Look, there are many open questions. In all conscience, I don't feel I can perform this wedding. But without a license, I couldn't even if I wanted to. Without a license, the state won't recognize the marriage. I'll probably be arrested for fraud.

CARMICHAEL/COHEN: What, for granting the last wish of a dying man? They'll lift you on their shoulders and carry you up the steps of city hall. You'll be a hero for performing a...what is it...you know...an act of goodness?

RABBI SCHECTER: A mitzvah.

CARMICHAEL/COHEN: That's it…a mitzvah. We're not just talking about a wedding here. This is a man's soul hanging in the balance. Show some compassion.

RABBI SCHECTER: *(A painful subject for him.)* Compassion? Do you think I have no compassion?

CARMICHAEL/COHEN: All I said was…

RABBI SCHECTER: I heard. Of all the things you might have said, you chose to mention my compassion. Or lack of it.

CARMICHAEL/COHEN: Well, I could use some right about now.

RABBI SCHECTER: Yes, a rabbi should have compassion. A respect for human needs and frailties. Compassion, I'm afraid, is not a great strength of mine. Even my wife says so. She says I'm too rigid and insensitive. Too concerned with the letter of the law and not enough with people. You sensed my failing, too.

SISTER VERONICA: Rabbi, this is not about you.

RABBI SCHECTER: In a way, it is. As odd as his story is, I have to…

SISTER VERONICA: Odd isn't the half of it.

CARMICHAEL/COHEN: Would you please knock it off, Sister Buttin-ski. Let the man say what's on his mind.

RABBI SCHECTER: As bizarre as his story is…

CARMICHAEL/COHEN: Aha. Before, my story was odd. She put her two cents in, and now it's bizarre.

RABBI SCHECTER: Let's just say it's unusual, then. Is that all right?

CARMICHAEL/COHEN: Why not? *(An afterthought.)* I'm an unusual person.

RABBI SCHECTER: Whatever this man's background, whatever his reasons, he is obviously serious about what he says. I have an obligation to pay attention to him, to show him…compassion.

CARMICHAEL/COHEN: Bravo.

SISTER VERONICA: Rabbi, you just walked in here a few minutes ago, and you know nothing of this man's history. I've been supervising his care for four weeks…this time. And he's been in this hospital twice before this, always, it seems, as my responsibility. He must have told me twenty different stories about who he is and where he came from. Today is the first time he ever claimed to be Jewish.

CARMICHAEL/COHEN: I had to give it a lot of thought first. You don't just suddenly sit up in bed at Our Lady of Mercy Hospital and holler out that you're a Jew.

SISTER VERONICA: *(Indignant.)* Meaning what? There are a number of Jewish patients here right now, and they receive the same consideration as anyone else.

CARMICHAEL/COHEN: Yeah? Just try and get a pastrami sandwich.

RABBI SCHECTER: We can't just dismiss what he says out of hand. How can we really know what's true and what's not? Spain and aristocratic Jews and a Pittsburgh insurance adjuster. A person doesn't just make these things up.

SISTER VERONICA: Oh, but he does. Faster than you can snap your fingers.

RABBI SCHECTER: Maybe so, but there's something significant going on inside this man. We must recognize that he's at a crucial point in his life. We have to show…compassion.

CARMICHAEL/COHEN: You can learn something, sister. Pick up a few pointers from Rabbi Samuels, here.

SISTER VERONICA: With all respect, rabbi, I'm not exactly a stranger to compassion. The whole mission of my life is serving Christ by helping to heal bodies and souls.

RABBI SCHECTER: I certainly don't mean to imply…

CARMICHAEL/COHEN: Aha! She heals souls! Don't you get it? Don't you see why she's trying to discredit me? If I die as a Jew, then she's lost me. She's failed.

SISTER VERONICA: That's where you're wrong. Those who die outside the Catholic church, it's they who lose. But you will not be lost, Mr. Carmichael.

CARMICHAEL/COHEN: How about that, rabbi? There's a paradise up there in the sky, but it's for Catholics only. Jews need not apply.

RABBI SCHECTER: That's something we probably shouldn't get into, right here and right now.

SISTER VERONICA: Yes. This discussion is moot. It's clear that Mr. Carmichael isn't…exactly…himself. What he says and does now, no matter how…bizarre…must be weighed against a lifetime as a devout Catholic. He doesn't truly mean it. God understands, I'm sure.

CARMICHAEL/COHEN: *(Sitting upright. Exploding.)* Just who the hell do you think you are, telling me what I mean? And how do you know what God understands? You're a nun, not a prophet. If I stay a good Catholic, well, that's OK with you, right? But if I decide I want to be a Jew, that's the aberration of a crazy old man, and it doesn't count. Huh? Huh? Either way, I'm going out as a Catholic. Heads you win, tails I lose. Well, that's BULLSHIT!

SISTER VERONICA: Please, I'm trying to explain…

CARMICHAEL/COHEN: *(Highly agitated.)* BULLSHIT! HI DIDDLE BULLSHIT, BULLSHIT, BULLSHIT! *(Suddenly, he appears to be stricken. He clutches at his chest and falls backward onto his pillow, gasping loudly for breath. He moans, more and more slowly. His eyes close. He is quiet. And still.)*

SISTER VERONICA: *(She goes to CARMICHAEL/COHEN and takes his pulse. She and RABBI SCHECTER look at each other fearfully.)* I can't feel anything.

RABBI SCHECTER: It was too much for him. Why did we put him through this? I just should have agreed…

SISTER VERONICA: *(Moving quickly toward the door.)* Let me run for the crash cart. We can still…

ESTHER: *(She is wearing a frumpy housedress. As she enters, she collides with SISTER VERONICA.)* For chrissakes. Watch where you're…*(Realizing that SISTER VERONICA is a nun, she cuts her comment short. She sees CARMICHAEL/COHEN lying motionless.)* What's with Eddie. Is he all right?

CARMICHAEL/COHEN: *(Sitting up and smiling.)* Esther, sweetheart!

ESTHER: Eddie. What is it, Eddie? What's wrong?

CARMICHAEL/COHEN: Now that you're here, nothing is wrong. Everything is hunky-dory.

ESTHER: Jesus, Eddie. The way you sounded on the phone, I thought you were on your way out. I ran down here so fast, I forgot and left my chicken in the oven.

CARMICHAEL/COHEN: You're such a love.

ESTHER: Why did you tell me to come in such a hurry?

SISTER VERONICA: *(To RABBI SCHECTER.)* You see? You see how he manipulates people. *(To ESTHER.)* He hasn't told you about his plan for you and him? No, I didn't think so.

ESTHER: What is it your business? This is between Eddie and me. *(Suspicious.)* What plan?

SISTER VERONICA: This man is a rabbi.

CARMICHAEL/COHEN: Rabbi Siegel.

RABBI SCHECTER: Schecter.

ESTHER: So?

SISTER VERONICA: *(To CARMICHAEL/COHEN.)* Tell her why she's here and why the rabbi's here.

CARMICHAEL/COHEN: Esther...my sweet...I've come to a decision...

RABBI SCHECTER: *(Seeing that CARMICHAEL/COHEN is having a hard time explaining.)* Go ahead. What's the problem?

ESTHER: My chicken is shrinking up to nothing while I'm standing here. What the hell is going on?

SISTER VERONICA: Mr. Carmichael?

CARMICHAEL/COHEN: *(After a difficult pause.)* My sweetheart, I know that because of the strong affection you and I have had for each other over these years...these wonderful years...the subject of marriage has come up more than once.

ESTHER: Yeah, you kept asking and I kept refusing.

CARMICHAEL/COHEN: And so I have decided to sanctify our relationship with holy matrimony. The rabbi is here to marry us.

ESTHER: What, are you kidding? You and me? Us?

CARMICHAEL/COHEN: I know we won't have long together as husband and wife. Only until tonight.

SISTER VERONICA: He seems to think he is departing this world tonight. But I would be much surprised if he weren't still here in the morning.

RABBI SCHECTER: Miz Goldman, I have to…

ESTHER: That's Mrs. Goldman. I was married twenty-seven years. I parted company with Mr. Goldman the loser eight years ago April. I said, face it Harry, there's no future anymore for a kosher butcher.

RABBI SCHECTER: Mrs. Goldman, it's terribly important that we understand what you and Mr. Cohen mean to each other.

ESTHER: Who's Mr. Cohen?

SISTER VERONICA: Mr. Carmichael claims that he is.

CARMICHAEL/COHEN: Tell them, Esther. Tell them I'm Eddie Cohen.

RABBI SCHECTER: It's vital that I know whether you want to marry him.

ESTHER: Can somebody please…

RABBI SCHECTER: And whether he is really Jewish or not.

ESTHER: *(With growing desperation.)* All right, I want you to tell me…

SISTER VERONICA: Mr. Carmichael is on strong medications, and he is simply not rational.

ESTHER: *(Louder.)* What I need to know here is why…

RABBI SCHECTER: There are important issues, which, as a responsible clergyman, I must address. And I believe that you are the…

ESTHER: *(Finally exploding.)* WOULD SOMEBODY PLEASE LET ME KNOW WHAT THE FUCK IS GOING ON HERE!

RABBI SCHECTER: This man claims that his name is not Carmichael, but Cohen. That he is not Catholic, but Jewish. And that he asked me to come here to officiate at his wedding with you. As he is seriously ill, I want to show…the compassion…which is appropriate….

ESTHER: Oh, rabbi, he's so full of shit. *(To CARMICHAEL/COHEN.)* Cohen? How do you come to be a Cohen?

CARMICHAEL/COHEN: *(To RABBI SCHECTER.)* The Cohens are the priests, right? The religious bluebloods. The aristocrats.

RABBI SCHECTER: Yes.

CARMICHAEL/COHEN: What else could I be?

ESTHER: Sure, Cohen.

CARMICHAEL/COHEN: Sweetheart, I don't have much time left. We can at least enjoy a few hours of wedded bliss.

ESTHER: You're lying there with a tube up your nose. How blissful could it be?

RABBI SCHECTER: You don't want to marry him, then?

ESTHER: I don't know what he's been telling you about us, because he's such a bullshit artist. Mind you, he's interesting, and he's fun. But he makes up stories. One minute he's a Russian prince, the next he's the bastard son of Dwight Eisenhower. Who knows?

SISTER VERONICA: And you've been friendly with him? Why have you put up with all his stories?

ESTHER: We've been extremely friendly…if you catch my drift. Every Wednesday night for six years. He lives in the apartment right below mine. So he'd take a stroll upstairs…

CARMICHAEL/COHEN: My stairway to paradise.

ESTHER: He's not a bad guy, really. Thoughtful, kind, entertaining. And until he got sick, a lot of sexual intensity for a man in his seventies. *(Shrugging.)* So he lies…a lot.

RABBI SCHECTER: You said he asked you to marry him before, and you refused him. Why?

ESTHER: Who needs it? Do I really want to spend my golden years making chicken soup for a sick old man? And, do you think that after a lifetime as a pious Jewish woman, I'm going to marry this Irish Catholic?

CARMICHAEL/COHEN: I'm Jewish, sweetheart. God's truth. I have plenty of Jewish blood in my veins. On my mother's side, where it counts.

SISTER VERONICA: So that's it. She won't marry you because you're not Jewish. So you decided to say you're a Jew.

CARMICHAEL/COHEN: As God is my witness, it's all true, every syllable.

ESTHER: Nice try, Eddie. Really, I'm flattered. You're such a lovely guy, I might almost be tempted. But no. You're not well, and you're not Jewish. You're a sick Catholic person.

CARMICHAEL/COHEN: You're breaking my heart. Well, I hoped it wouldn't come to this, but now I have one more thing I must reveal to you.

SISTER VERONICA: Oh, save us. Here it comes.

CARMICHAEL/COHEN: You know I live modestly. I'm not a rich man. But I did put away some money years ago, before I retired. I have no living relatives, no heirs and no will. I want to leave that money to my wife…to you. Seventy-nine thousand dollars, Esther. And it's yours.

ESTHER: *(Outraged.)* You putz, I can't believe what I'm hearing. Are you trying to bribe me to marry you?

CARMICHAEL/COHEN: God forbid. I'm simply trying to show you how much you mean to me…how much I love you. What's wrong with that?

ESTHER: I don't need your money.

CARMICHAEL/COHEN: I know you don't need it, but I want you to have it. Marry me, lover.

SISTER VERONICA: Where did you get all that money? From your family in Vienna or the one in Spain? And where is it, stuffed in your mattress?

CARMICHAEL/COHEN: What! You're doubting me? There's a CD in the First Federal Bank, just laying there gathering interest. Ninety-four thousand dollars.

RABBI SCHECTER: You just said seventy-nine thousand dollars.

CARMICHAEL/COHEN: I told you it was gathering interest.

SISTER VERONICA: Then why don't you just give the money to this woman, or write a will and leave it to her? Why must she marry you to get it?

CARMICHAEL/COHEN: Oh, no. This money is for my wife. No wife…the bank will give the money to the government, and they'll do what they do with money that doesn't belong to anyone.

RABBI SCHECTER: Which is?

CARMICHAEL/COHEN: They'll piss it away.

ESTHER: Eddie, you're putting me in a hell of a position. I feel for you, you know that. But do you want everybody to think I married you for money? And besides, I can't marry out of my religion. So that's that.

CARMICHAEL/COHEN: Hi diddle diddle, so you're in the middle. Rabbi, tell her I'm Jewish. You know the truth.

RABBI SCHECTER: The truth I'm not so sure of. But he does claim to be Jewish on his mother's side.

CARMICHAEL/COHEN: You won't have to make me chicken soup, I promise. One simple "I do," a final few hours of two hearts beating as one, and whoops…you're a widow. A rich widow.

ESTHER: Oh, stop it.

CARMICHAEL/COHEN: Don't deny me this, sweetheart. There's very little left to me in this world, and I'm getting to the end. Marrying me is an act of love, a…a…what is it?

RABBI SCHECTER: A mitzvah.

CARMICHAEL/COHEN: That's it. Do this thing and you'll be blessed forever. Help me make sense of it all. I've led a virtuous life…

SISTER VERONICA: As a good Catholic.

CARMICHAEL/COHEN: Always knowing, down deep, that I was a Jew. Listen, do you think for a minute I didn't know about my aristocratic Jewish forebears in Argentina?

SISTER VERONICA: Oh, it's Argentina. now?

CARMICHAEL/COHEN: By way of England, as I have already explained.

SISTER VERONICA: Enough of this. It can go no further.

RABBI SCHECTER: Well now, just a minute. Perhaps this situation is not quite so clear-cut as it seems.

SISTER VERONICA: *(Astonished.)* Whatever do you mean?

ESTHER: You mean you think he's really Jewish, like he says?

RABBI SCHECTER: I think he thinks he's Jewish. I think he loves you. I think he believes he wants to leave you money.

SISTER VERONICA: Are we not to be concerned with the truth here? What this man believes and what is so, are two vastly different things. He's taking three different kinds of medication. Any of them are powerful enough to cause him to see the angel of death walk by in a tweed sport jacket.

CARMICHAEL/COHEN: Brown, it was. Three button. Kind of a herringbone.

RABBI SCHECTER: I'm not so sure any of that matters. I think what matters is what he believes. And if we care at all for this man, then perhaps we shouldn't challenge him, but rather pay him the respect of accepting the world as he would like it to be. That's not much to ask.

CARMICHAEL/COHEN: This is my kind of rabbi.

SISTER VERONICA: What must be respected here is a lifetime spent as a Catholic. If his senses were clear, he'd never give up his religion now, so close to the end.

CARMICHAEL/COHEN: Bullshit.

ESTHER: Rabbi, what are you thinking? What should we do here?

RABBI SCHECTER: I believe the answer is simple. Standing here, it's been revealed to me, quite plainly, from the depths of my own memory.

ESTHER: What are you talking about?

RABBI SCHECTER: I have to tell you about my father's sister, my Aunt Sylvia. I was just a small boy, but I remember her very well. A lovely, sweet woman, clever and funny and always quick to laugh.

SISTER VERONICA: Excuse me, rabbi, but what does this have to do with…

RABBI SCHECTER: I'll explain. Please be patient. When Aunt Sylvia was in her late sixties, her mental processes began to fail. I guess today they'd call it Alzheimers, but then they called it senility. Sometimes she didn't recognize people. Or she mixed them up. She started to call me Fievel…Philip…which was the name of my older brother, who had died of tuberculosis years earlier. And her husband, my Uncle Zack, she thought he was her father, Grandpa Schecter, who was gone already thirty years, long before I was born. She called her husband "papa," and she'd ask him to play games with her. This infuriated Uncle Zack, who had the reputation in our family of being a loudmouth and a bully. He'd hold her by the wrists and shout at her, "I'm your husband. I'm your husband." Oh, he was fierce. Of course, Aunt Sylvia couldn't understand, and she'd pull away and run into the bathroom and lock the door.

SISTER VERONICA: This is not the same situation…

CARMICHAEL/COHEN: Would you let him tell the story, please.

ESTHER: Yes, go on.

RABBI SCHECTER: She got worse, and Uncle Zack couldn't take care of her any more, so he put her in a home. For a while, she seemed to be happier there. She could walk reasonably well, so they used to let her push other patients around in their wheelchairs. One day, an old man she pushed in his chair disappeared. They asked her if she knew what had become of him, but she couldn't understand the question. After a whole day of looking, they finally found him. Aunt Sylvia had pushed him into a broom closet and left him there, sitting in the dark. He was scared and dehydrated, but he survived. After that, though, no more wheelchair duty for her. She lost her sense of purpose, and she went downhill fast. Uncle Zack would come to see her and lose his temper whenever she called him papa. There'd be a scene, and the poor woman would end up whimpering like a beaten dog, wretched and miserable, while Uncle Zack stormed out of the place. My father took me to the home just before she died. By that time she had shriveled up to become a tiny little woman. Through all of her illness, my father was the only one she always recognized. She called him Moish...for Morris. I remember, that day, she said to him, with tears running down her cheeks, "Moish, papa doesn't love me anymore."

SISTER VERONICA: *(After a long pause.)* What a terrible thing.

RABBI SCHECTER: Can you imagine, being deathly sick and believing that your father has forsaken you? Of course, it wasn't so. But the point is, in Aunt Sylvia's...dementia...she thought it was. If only Uncle Zack would have said to her, when she called him papa, "You're my precious daughter, and I love you dearly." Would it have killed him?

CARMICHAEL/COHEN: The son-of-a-bitch.

ESTHER: Son-of-a-bitch bastard.

SISTER VERONICA: And so?

ESTHER: He's saying, if we do what Eddie wants, would it kill us?

CARMICHAEL/COHEN: Yeah, would it kill you?

RABBI SCHECTER: Maybe none of it is real. Maybe he's a Catholic and maybe he's a Jew. Maybe there's no money. Maybe the state won't recognize the marriage, and maybe God won't, either. I don't know. I only know there is a good soul here looking for peace, time is running out…and we mustn't turn away.

ESTHER: You're right.

SISTER VERONICA: You're not saying you're going to go through with this? But it's a lie. A falsehood before God.

RABBI SCHECTER: God will understand. God has compassion. And charity.

SISTER VERONICA: But we don't have the…

RABBI SCHECTER: "And now abideth faith, hope charity, these three: but the greatest of these is charity."

SISTER VERONICA: New Testament, Rabbi?

RABBI SCHECTER: I try to keep an open mind. Sister, can't we be charitable here? If we allow this man some joy, who will be harmed by it?

SISTER VERONICA: None of what you're saying changes the fact that…

CARMICHAEL/COHEN: Come on, Sister.

ESTHER: Would it kill you?

RABBI SCHECTER: "The greatest of these is charity."

SISTER VERINICA: Charity? And what, exactly, do you want us to give this man?

RABBI SCHECTER: The benefit of the doubt.

SISTER VERONICA: *(After a long, thoughtful pause.)* Very well.

RABBI SCHECTER: *(To ESTHER.)* What more is there to say? Are you ready?

ESTHER: To get married? Just like that? Dressed in this schmatte?

RABBI SCHECTER: It's fine, believe me. Just stand over there, next to the bed.

CARMICHAEL/COHEN: No, no. I'm not going to get married on my back. I have to be on my own two feet. Would you help me up…Sister Veronica?

> *With great effort SISTER VERONICA gets CARMICHAEL/ COHEN to his feet, and supports him. ESTHER stands next to him.*

ESTHER: I can't believe this.

CARMICHAEL/COHEN: This is the happiest day of my life. If only my family from France were here.

SISTER VERONICA: Don't start.

RABBI SCHECTER: Let's begin.

ESTHER: Wait! *(She goes to the flowers, takes them out of the vase and shakes the water from the stems. Holding them as a bridal bouquet, she returns to CARMICHAEL/COHEN's side.)* Now.

RABBI SCHECTER: We are gathered here in the sight of God to join together in holy matrimony Esther Goldman, and…Eddie Cohen.

> *Blackout.*

ARE YOU JEWISH?

THE CHARACTERS

Sonny Simmons, weather reporter for a cable channel

Rose Glassman, a woman in her 60s

The Director, a voice on a loudspeaker

THE TIME

Night

THE PLACE

A local cable television studio

As the lights fade up, SONNY SIMMONS, a weather reporter for a local cable channel, is beginning her weathercast. As she speaks to her cable audience, she refers to a weather map which is electronically "matted in" behind her, and which we, of course, cannot see. She is trying hard to win her audience over, and is far more cheerful and effusive than the situation, and the weather, warrant. She does her best to make even bad weather sound good, and she always smiles.

SONNY: Yes, there were a few periods of patchy rain today...but compared to yesterday...well, much nicer, all in all. It's true, there were some areas to the north and west that experienced a period of downpour late this afternoon, and there was some local flooding. But it cleared up just beautifully, and all the roads are open now...except for I-63, State Roads 25 and 48, route 67 between Lyle and Mechanicsburg, and both approaches to the Millard Fillmore Bridge. *(With an especially broad smile.)* Well, that's early spring for you, isn't it? You know what they say...April showers bring May flowers. *(Laughing brightly.)* All right, let's look ahead, because we're expecting a bright future, weatherwise. We can anticipate a long stretch of sunshine, and temperatures reaching into the high 60s...or maybe even the 70s...*(Gesturing at the unseen weather map behind her.)*...right after this broad cold front blowing down from mid-Canada works it's way through our area. Today there were strong winds...well, gale force, actually...over the Great Lakes, and a report of heavy snow in the western corner of the state. Of course, as we all know, there's apt to be snow in the mountains right into May, isn't there? Anyway, for us right here tomorrow and Wednesday, and probably through Thursday, our weather will be, well, unsettled. So watch Jack Mulligan on "Good Morning, Neighbors" starting at 5:30 tomorrow morning, for school closings. *(Another big smile.)* But you know what? The last gasp of winter will be gone before we know it. Then it's right into spring and on to summer. Backyard barbecues and picnics, swimming and suntans and baseball. It's all just around the corner.

> *ROSE GLASSMAN moves quietly into the studio. She waves discretely at SONNY, who is startled at the appearance of a stranger in the studio.*

SONNY: *(Gesturing.)* Uh…for tomorrow, then, we can expect strong winds beginning shortly after sunrise. Plus the possibility of snow flurries…with drifting up to eighteen inches. Uh…but as I said, these clouds have a silver lining. I'll be back with the Cable 12s five-day forecast right after these messages. *(As the channel cuts away for a commercial break, she speaks to ROSE. Though she is puzzled and concerned by ROSE's presence, her smile never leaves her face.)* Yes? Who are you?

ROSE: Hello, darling. Oh my, you're even prettier in person than you are on the television.

SONNY: What are you doing here? What do you want?

ROSE: I'm Rose Glassman, darling. But call me Rose. You have beautiful cheekbones, you know that? The television doesn't do your cheekbones justice. They should fix the lighting. Who's the head person?

SONNY: What do you want? I'm in the middle of a broadcast.

ROSE: Don't worry about me. You go right ahead. I'll talk to the lighting person.

SONNY: How did you get in?

ROSE: Nobody stopped me. The door was open. The studio's empty except for you. I walked in.

SONNY: I'm afraid you can't stay.

ROSE: We see you every night, me and my son Norman…except on the weekends when that colored girl is on. *(Showing a framed photo from her purse.)* This is my Norman. Such a good-looking boy, don't you think? We're very big fans. Believe me, nobody in your audience is as devoted as we are. We think you're a very special person.

SONNY: That's kind of you, but what do you want? The break is almost half over. I have to finish. People are waiting for my five-day forecast.

ROSE: Not really.

SONNY: What?

ROSE: A weather forecast they can get anyplace. What they're really waiting for is another look at you. Oh, this is a real doll-face.

SONNY: But could you please explain what you want?

ROSE: What's to explain? A handsome boy. A beautiful girl. You don't have to be a Dick Tracy to reach a conclusion.

SONNY: This is all very nice, really, but I…

ROSE: You know what my Norman says every time you come on? "What a wonderful girl. Always so cheerful. I could fall in love with a girl like that."

SONNY: Please…

ROSE: So I told him, "Call her up. Say hello. Invite her out for lunch. She'd like a lunch in a nice restaurant. These people on local cable don't get paid that much that they eat in fancy places." But he didn't call because he was shy. I tried to call you myself, but you were never here. Then I thought to myself, you'll have to come to do the weather…so here I am now. But listen, what's a mother for?

> *The director's voice is heard on a speaker from the control booth. "Coming back now. Five seconds…four…"*

SONNY: The break is over. We're going live. You really have to leave, because you can't…

ROSE: Sonny Simmons…this is your real name?

SONNY: *(Aware that she is back on the air. Gesturing.)* We're back with the five-day forecast. Tomorrow look for a low temperature of 28 and a high of 33. Of course it could always go higher. Strong winds and snow, heavy at times…unless it just blows over. Sometimes it does that. A warming trend will begin Wednesday, with a high of 35, and, up a full two degrees. Snow flurries will continue. On Thursday…

ROSE: You don't look like somebody who has a name Sonny Simmons.

SONNY: *(Trying to maintain her composure, and ignore ROSE.)*…the snow should stop before noon, with clear skies expected by mid-afternoon. The temperature will reach into…

ROSE: Are you Jewish?

SONNY: …uh…into the high 40s before sunset, for a calm, pleasant evening. And…uh…get ready for a spring weekend that's really special, starting on Friday as…uh…

ROSE: The very first time I saw you, I said to myself, this is a Jewish girl. I can tell. That's why I encouraged Norman.

SONNY: …a warm front moves up from the southern states. We'll be enjoying sunny days right through Saturday…

ROSE: *(Moving close to SONNY, into the television picture.)* You know, you look a lot like Flora Pechman's daughter…maybe you know her…Jennifer? Also very shiksa cheekbones.

SONNY: *(Rattled, but still smiling.)* Well, as you can see, we have a visitor in our Cable 12 studio tonight. Uh…welcome…

ROSE: And the nose, too. Beautiful. But of course everybody knows Jennifer Pechman's nose is not her own. You have the nose you were born with. I can tell.

SONNY: Well, now…uh…let's look into our weather history and find the record temperatures for March 28. The record high was 67, and that was back in 1949…

ROSE: So you're going to tell me?

SONNY: And…uh…in 1974, the record low temperature for this day was just 13 degrees. Imagine that, just 13….

ROSE: So? Am I right or am I right?

SONNY: *(Seriously rattled. Her smile fades.)* What? What?

ROSE: You're Jewish, am I correct?

SONNY: This is really not the time. There are thousands of people watching.

ROSE: Including my Norman. *(To the TV audience.)* Hello, Norman. Here I am, and I'm taking care of everything. She's a lovely girl. And I was right about her. Up close, there's no mistaking.

SONNY: *(Trying to regain control of the situation.)* And in…uh…1938, there was over 14 inches of snow on this day. And that's Cable 12 weather.

ROSE: You're Jewish, I know.

SONNY: Look, Mrs.…Mrs…

ROSE: Glassman. Rose Glassman. Like I said, call me Rose.

SONNY: Look, Mrs…Rose, what I am has nothing to do with…*(Looking up to the director's booth.)* I'm off, right?

DIRECTOR'S VOICE ON SPEAKER: No, you're still on.

SONNY: Why? The weather's over. *(A forced smile to the television audience.)*

DIRECTOR'S VOICE ON SPEAKER: Phonecalls are coming in from everywhere. They love this. Everybody wants to see how it turns out.

SONNY: No, I don't want to do this. This is crazy. *(Another smile to the audience.)*

DIRECTOR'S VOICE ON SPEAKER: The whole town's watching. The boss says keep going. Valuable publicity.

SONNY: Kill this camera and start the movie. If you don't, I'll walk right out of here.

DIRECTOR'S VOICE ON SPEAKER: Don't do it Sonny. This is a big opportunity. Think about it. It'll be in all the papers. Great for us, great for your career. Anyway, the boss says keep going.

SONNY: I'm the weather reporter. There's nothing that says I have to stand here while people wander into the studio and start asking me personal questions while I'm on the air. *(Smiling and looking to the TV audience.)* Isn't that right? Do I have to be embarrassed this way?

ROSE: Oh, now, darling, don't get upset. It's not in my nature to embarrass anyone.

SONNY: Would you please leave.

ROSE: Listen, if you want me to go, then I'm going. But before I leave, I want to invite you to our house for dinner. Friday night. It'll be so nice. You and Norman can get to know each other, and I'll make a real shabbos meal. What do you say?

SONNY: I couldn't possibly do that.

ROSE: Of course you could. Don't be shy. Listen, what have you got to lose? You'll meet an eligible young man who's very…how should I say…smitten with you already. And besides that, I promise you a wonderful dinner.

SONNY: I am not coming to your house for dinner Friday…or any night.

ROSE: I will make for you a shabbos dinner to remember. What are your favorite things? How about some nice gedemte brisket? Oh, and I'll make a potato kugel. I'm famous for my potato kugel. And…just because it's you…I'll bake a fresh challah. So…how could you refuse?

SONNY: I've never eaten any of those things in my life.

ROSE: What? Of course you have. Maybe not as good as mine, but…

SONNY: Never.

DIRECTOR'S VOICE ON SPEAKER: Go to the dinner. The boss says go to dinner with her.

SONNY: Let *him* go to dinner with her.

DIRECTOR'S VOICE ON SPEAKER: He says a good potato kugel would be worth the trip.

SONNY: Mrs. Glassman…

ROSE: Rose.

SONNY: All right, all right. Rose…you have this all wrong.

ROSE: What do you mean, wrong?

SONNY: You think…you believe I'm a Jewish person, don't you?

ROSE: Of course. *(After a stunned pause.)* You mean you're not?

SONNY: No. I'm a Lutheran. From Fargo, North Dakota.

ROSE: But your name. Nobody has a name Sonny Simmons.

SONNY: *(Resigned, throwing up her hands.)* OK, what the hell. No more smiling. You're right, Rose. That name I just made up. You want to know what my real name is?

ROSE: Yes, I do.

DIRECTOR'S VOICE ON SPEAKER: Everybody does.

SONNY: *(After a pause.)* Emily…Rothenbucher. OK? Is my life over, or is there still hope for me?

ROSE: Oh, darling, I'm so sorry.

SONNY: Which part don't you like? Emily…or Rothenbucher?

ROSE: Darling, you have a…well, a lovely name. Of course. But I just assumed…I mean, I'm never wrong. But now I'm wrong. Right?

SONNY: Wrong doesn't begin to cover it.

ROSE: Oy.

SONNY: *(Gesturing at the TV audience,)* Not only are you wrong, but the whole world knows it.

ROSE: Please forgive me. I'm sorry I bothered you. And of course, you don't have to come on Friday night.

SONNY: What are you saying?

ROSE: I know you don't want to come. Now I understand.

SONNY: You're *un*-inviting me? Now you're telling me I *shouldn't* come?

ROSE: I'm just saying, as I was wrong about your being Jewish, there's really no reason for you and Norman to meet.

SONNY: What!

ROSE: Well…a Jewish boy and a…*(Seeing that SONNY is glaring at her.)*…girl from North Dakota…

SONNY: A *Lutheran* girl from North Dakota.

ROSE: That, too.

SONNY: Let me get this straight. You sneak in here while I'm on the air. You make a mess of my program. You embarrass me in front of the entire planet. You force me to reveal things that are nobody's business but my own. And now…guess what?…I'm not good enough for your son?

ROSE: I never said that. All I'm saying is…

SONNY: You and your son…uh…

ROSE: Norman.

SONNY: You and Norman…you're some kind of Jewish royalty, then? And what am I, a nobody…because I'm not Jewish? Somebody your son shouldn't associate with, because maybe, just maybe, it we might like each other?

ROSE: Listen, darling…

SONNY: Don't "Listen, darling" me.

DIRECTOR'S VOICE ON SPEAKER: Sonny, there's someone on the phone says he's Norman Glassman. He says please come to dinner, and he'll deal with his mother.

SONNY: You hear that, Rose Glassman? So there's *somebody* in your family who's not a bigot.

ROSE: Me? A bigot? God forbid. *(To the television audience.)* All right, Norman. There's no need to humiliate me further. I see which way the wind is blowing. *(To SONNY.)* So you'll come Friday, then? And I'll make maybe a nice meat loaf with brown gravy, peas and carrots, something like that.

SONNY: Oh, no you don't.

ROSE: You don't like meat loaf?

SONNY: No, I want that…whatchamacallit brisket…and the potato…thing. Or I'm not coming.

ROSE: The challah, too?

SONNY: Absolutely. What is it?

DIRECTOR'S VOICE ON SPEAKER: Sonny, the phonecalls are backed up like you wouldn't believe. Everybody wants you to go to dinner with her. And listen to this: the Associated Press just called. They want an interview.

ROSE: I'm so thrilled for you, darling. Friday night, then?

SONNY: Friday night.

ROSE: And you'll forgive me, can I ask you just one more question?

SONNY: What!

ROSE: The last one, I promise. I never pry.

SONNY: What is it?

ROSE: What does your father do?

Blackout.

ABOUT THE AUTHOR

BRUCE J. BLOOM, Playwright—

Bloom's plays have entertained audiences throughout Westchester County, NY, on Long Island, in the Midwest and as far away as New Zealand. He has directed many productions for local theatres, is seen on stage often, and was drama critic for *The Scarsdale Inquirer.*

978-0-595-36123-6
0-595-36123-4